Ismail Merchant's
Indian Cuisine

Ismail Merchant's Indian Cuisine

Futura

A Futura Book

Copyright© Ismail Merchant 1986
Photography by Meryl Joseph.

First published in Great Britain in 1986 by Futura
Publications, a Division of Macdonald & Co (Publishers) Ltd
London & Sydney

ISBN 0 7088 2876 0

Typeset by Leaper & Gard Ltd, Bristol
Printed in Great Britain by The Guernsey Press

The publishers would like to thank James Ivory, Richard Robbins,
Anthony Korner, Simon Callow, Sarah Fox-Pitt, Felicity Kendal
and Sandra Korner for their contributions to Indian Cuisine.
They would also like to thank Scott Ewing for his editorial work.

Futura Publications
A Division of
Macdonald & Co (Publishers) Ltd
Maxwell House
74 Worship Street
London EC2A 2EN
A BPCC plc Company

Contents

Acknowledgements   *page*   1

Introduction   3

Some Friends Comment ...   12

Hors d'oeuvres and drinks   23

Soups   31

Fish   45

Poultry and Eggs   69

Meat   103

Vegetables   133

Salads   163

Rice   177

Pulses   189

Sweets   199

Pickles and Chutneys   215

Index   229

Index of Indian Titles   233

For Ammi and Abba

Acknowledgments

It is a simple thing to tell one's friends, 'I am writing a cook book,' but doing so has turned out to be a very painstaking and meticulous operation, even something of a chore, which for me actual cooking never is. So in trying to put this all together I often became very impatient. My approach to cooking has always been pragmatic and experimental (not so different really from the way I go about finding the finance for my films).

This book wouldn't have been possible without the help of my colleague and friend, Dick Robbins, who composed the music for several of our recent films, from *The Europeans* to *A Room With A View*. He has gone through every recipe, testing ones he wasn't familiar with, and then arranging them, ingredient by ingredient, instruction by instruction, for the whole book. I don't think I could have got through without his attention to tiny details, something essential for any successful recipe.

Going back further, I must thank Jim Ivory not only for his encouragement in this present venture, but for his patience when, after a hard day, it was easier to make *Qeema* (minced meat) than *Adrak aur shazeera walli ran* (roast lamb), or to warm up some *dal*, rather than to shop for all the tasty treats he so looks forward to.

I would like to thank Scott Ewing, a freelance editor I met through my publisher, who rechecked all the recipes, testing many of them, and prepared the final text of the recipes for the printers. I am also grateful to Begum Sabeeha Ahmed Husain for helping me with suggestions of Indian names for the recipes.

Finally, my thanks to Ruth Prawer Jhabvala, who has eaten my food with enthusiasm and encouraged me by her amazed comments on the speed with which I conjure up a meal.

Introduction

My friends say that my cooking is different from anything they have known. They call me a master chef and encourage me repeatedly to write a cookery book, a difficult undertaking as most of my time is spent making films. At last I relent and herein present some of my recipes, ideas on cooking and several stories about and from friends who have enjoyed my cooking — a section of stories from my friends follows this introduction.

So what makes a master chef? For me it means that he or she must have imagination, a flair for mixing conventional and unconventional ingredients, an appreciation of different seasonings and a desire for praise to satisfy his or her ego. A great cook should be able to do something well with the snap of a finger rather than to toil over it. He or she should be inventive, be someone who can whip up something from nothing. From two pieces of straw a master should be able to make a grand salad — well almost.

Now, you may not ever want to be a master chef, but anyone can learn certain techniques and basic methods which will produce delicious dishes. I have taught quite a few of my friends to do so. And some of you may even have a great talent waiting to be awakened. If this book inspires you, that's splendid; I want to help you please others by showing you how to cook delicious dishes for them, quickly and with as much ease as possible. My greatest challenge is to encourage you through my recipes to be adventurous and not be afraid to make discoveries. The tightrope act of whipping up a meal for several important guests in half an hour can be saved for later!

My own knowledge of food and cooking developed gradually. I was born into a middle-class family in Bombay, with six sisters, all of whom are superb cooks. My father never cooked, but he appreciates good food. Men were generally not allowed in the kitchen, so male family members never had an opportunity actually to cook. In India when I was growing up most middle-class families had a cook as well as someone to do the shopping. My mother supervised everything, though she too was and still is

3

a first-rate cook. I could freely invite twenty guests home and everything would be provided for, the most perfect menu with eight or ten dishes. But I could only appreciate the meal, never be directly involved.

Before leaving India I became familiar with Chinese cooking, but in America I learned about French, Italian and many other fine culinary traditions. I would often go to a small French restaurant that I could afford on 9th Avenue and 55th Street in Manhattan, The Brittany, have dinner and talk to the people there about food. Later, I spent a lot of time in France. Consequently, my cooking is not always purely Indian. Sometimes it is a combination of French and Indian. There are definitely some lighter elements in it from *Nouvelle Cuisine.* By the same token, when I make a spaghetti sauce, it's Italo-Indian. As with every chef my cooking is the result of many influences, but it remains essentially Indian.

It was in America that I actually learned to cook. As an Indian host I could not offer my guests hamburgers and hot dogs. They expected something more exotic. Saeed and Madhur Jaffrey were among the first to taste my cooking. Madhur wasn't cooking much then and in a way she and I were in the same boat. We wanted to recreate in New York City the Indian flavours we had grown up with. I remember one of the first meals I prepared for them when Saeed brought Madhur from the hospital with their first born, Zia. I prepared it in their tiny apartment on West 27th Street with O.Henry's ghost hovering around the kitchen. Saeed had warned me that occasionally the ghost appeared and I was convinced that my cooking disturbed his simple palate.

So in 1958, wanting to please my American friends, I learned how to do all the things I was not allowed to do in India: the cooking, all the shopping and the serving. In the U.S. one has to do everything and it is best if you enjoy it; fortunately I do. I discovered that my cooking developed into more than just a way to please my friends. It helped me make headway in my profession. I have invited writers, actors, financiers, bankers and all sorts of interesting — and useful — people involved in all aspects of film-making home for dinner. I like to think that my cooking and the occasion softened some of them up a bit.

A successful evening is one in which your guests experience something unique. Naturally you want a spectacular success, with guests heaping you with compliments before they wander off happily into the night. I maintain that this is possible without days, or even a day, of preparation. Part of a good cook's success, as I have said, has to do with speed.

One summer evening after a concert I invited some guests (of the useful sort) home for a late supper. I first served them wine — never mixed drinks, which would confuse their palates and other senses. I also served some poppadoms; then excused myself because I wanted to start cooking. They became quite panicky, glancing nervously at watches and suggesting it might, after all, be best to go to a restaurant. I insisted, 'Enjoy a glass of wine, and in half an hour everything will be ready.' They didn't seem very reassured. Earlier, however, I had bought striped bass, broccoli and salad ingredients and already had plenty of rice. Within half an hour I appeared from the kitchen with the four dishes. My guests could not believe that all this could be prepared so quickly, including refilling their glasses, darting in for some quick conversation, darting out for some essential phone calls, organizing background music, more poppadoms and so on. It was, they all told me, a memorable evening.

For years I never dared mention to my mother and sisters that I had learned to cook. I never told them that I could make something very nice in half an hour. But when I was visiting Bombay a few years ago, one day my mother wasn't feeling well. My sister Rukhsana had brought some huge prawns home and I told her I wanted to do something with them 'in the French style'. Telling everybody to relax in the sitting room, I shut myself in the kitchen. I cooked the prawns in a mustard sauce, which isn't actually so foreign for Indians; Bengalis cook seafood and fish in a mustard sauce every day. I noticed my sister looking through a crack in the kitchen door and overheard her telling the others that I was going to make a mess or burn myself, but in less than fifteen minutes, I brought the huge prawns out, serving them as an hors d'oeuvre.

Everyone was surprised and pleased, if somewhat alarmed, at my revelation of this new talent, for in orthodox Indian households the men of the family definitely stay out of the kitchen. My sister Rukhsana did say the prawns were not prepared as well as she would have done; they were not pure Indian but in an 'adulterated' style. However, she confessed that she loved eating them. After a little while she asked me, 'What did you put in it?'

Since then I have cooked many times for my family, though it is still hard for the women to get used to the idea that I can cook something delicious so quickly. It still seems a little beyond their imagination, but now, whenever I want to use their kitchen, they go into the sitting room and pretend to relax.

As a child my time in the kitchen was spent urging whoever was cooking to hurry up with their preparations. I had no idea then that cooking would later interest me so much. I was simply hungry and wanted to eat. When I came home from school for the noon-time break, I could smell the wonderful aromas coming from the kitchen as I ran up the stairs. As we had only one hour to go home, eat lunch and return to school, I would immediately begin agitating in the kitchen, growling and stomping about. The cooks would say they were trying to hurry, but they never changed their pattern of cooking, no matter how much I urged. Everything took a certain amount of time, and I had to wait. If I wanted to go back to school hungry, I was welcome to do that.

For lunch there would usually be fish, rice, bread, vegetables and *dal.* Pomfret was the favourite fish, often cooked with a coconut sauce. I preferred fish because it doesn't take as long as meat or chicken. These latter took longer to cook and, in my schoolboy opinion, were best served at night. Weekends were different; then the major meal was at mid-day.

When I return to Bombay, I always visit the market where I shopped as a child with my father. I go to look for fresh seasonal vegetables and fruit and to enjoy the spectacle and aroma of fresh produce — fish, meat and spices. Though it is one of the most pleasurable things to do in the city, it is a pity that few foreigners ever visit the huge Crawford Market in Bombay, an area modelled on London's Covent Garden. Now Covent Garden is a centre of designer boutiques and smart restaurants, where the only vegetables you'll see are in *ragoûts*, but the great stone and cast-iron structure that houses Crawford Market is still a very active place of commerce. Its vendors sit in a beautiful light filtered down from high skylights, making their vegetables and fruits look like jewels. The vendors preside over their stalls like so many Aladdins, a funny mixture of an Oriental bazaar and nineteenth-century England.

In London today, if you shop in Berwick Street in Soho or another open market with its pyramids of cabbages and so forth, you get something of the flavour of shopping in the bazaar in Bombay. But any market which has an attractive display of fresh vegetables and fruit is superior to the general supermarket. I'm sure part of the success of the Korean fruit and vegetable stands in Manhattan is the visual impression of heaped-up yet artfully arranged goods not unlike the displays found in good florists (and not unlike in price, either).

Now some words on kitchens and equipment. My own tiny kitchen must be one of New York's smallest. If readers were to see it, they might disbelieve my claims of having effortlessly tossed off the little dinner parties for which I have become well known. The kitchen measures 1.7 × 2.4 m (5½ × 8 ft) and has no other equipment than a four-ring gas stove and an oven. My little dinner parties *do* cost something in effort, and timing is all important, but restricted kitchen space is almost an Indian tradition. Most Indian cooks prepare superb meals of many dishes crouched over a spirit-burner set on the floor. There are no modern microwave ovens in Indian kitchens, not even in a rich man's house. A cook usually makes do with a two-burner gas stove, shifting the pots backwards and forwards as need arises. It's a bit like that in New York. The kitchens in the house in upstate New York and in my flat in London are different affairs, but like millions of other New Yorkers, I have to make do in a sort of broom closet, and have been doing so for twenty years.

Once I imported a proper English gas cooker into India so my mother and sisters would not have to squat on the floor in traditional fashion. They could stand to cook or even sit in front of it, but the cooker stood unused in a corner, covered with a khaki cloth until it was finally sold to neighbours. I don't think they ever used it much either.

Except for a food processor, I have very basic cooking utensils. The food processor has helped me to create certain dishes and to do some traditional chores with great ease and speed. Though it's a very good kitchen tool, and fun too, it is not a necessity. Whenever I mention combining ingredients in a food processor or blender, I know that the ingredients can be combind by hand instead. It simply takes longer. My other cooking utensils include three or four saucepans of various sizes; a few frying pans, all with covers; sharp knives; a grater for ginger, and a chopping board.

It's the ingredients, not the equipment, that should be special and the way you combine them. My own larder includes bay leaves, Dijon and coarse-grained mustards, good tarragon vinegar, vegetable oil for cooking and good olive oil for salads, and a ready collection of dried spices from which I make up my *masala* — or seasoning — mixtures. Sometimes these mixtures include items such as green chillies, parsley, coconut and coriander which I buy fresh for the occasion. Whether or not my *masalas* contain fresh ingredients, I always mix them on the spot before I start cooking. Apart from marinades, I think that too much advance preparation spoils the flavours of spice mixtures. There follows a list of what I consider the most important spices to have on hand. Other spices and ingredients I use in this book are available in most Indian shops if not in your local super-market.

Black pepper
Kali mirch

should be bought whole as peppercorns and freshly ground. I use it liberally in almost all of my cooking.

Caraway seeds
Shazeera

are gathered from a plant native to both Asia and Europe. This spice is used mostly in North Indian cooking. It's best to grind the seeds a little in a pestle and mortar just before using them to bring out their flavour.

Cardamom
Elaichi

comes in two basic types, the smaller pale green or white pods and the larger black or 'wild' pods. Sometimes the tiny black seeds are removed from the pods and crushed to use in cooking, but I usually use the whole pods in my recipes; it's easier. People just leave them on the side of their plate.

Cayenne pepper
Lal mirch

also called 'red chilli powder' in Indian grocers is basic to Indian cooking. I've used modest amounts of it in my recipes, so you may prefer to add more, once you taste the dish.

Garlic
Lasson

During the cold season my mother always made a bread with fresh green garlic as it provides warmth and comfort. In the West, garlic is not used so freely as it has a very strong aroma. People tend to avoid you when you have eaten a garlicky meal, so it is not a time to try and get close to somebody. In India, this prejudice is absent.I love garlic in my food and particularly use it with lentil dishes, for which I make *baghar*, frying chopped garlic in oil until it browns. Add it as a garnish.

Ginger
Adrak

is a knobbly growth on the root, not the root itself. Sometimes I don't bother, but its thin skin should really be peeled before grating or chopping, especially in a purée. Rarely if ever do I use dried ground ginger.

Mustard seeds
Sarson

Both yellow and black mustard seeds are used in Indian cooking. I prefer the black ones because of the way they look in a dish, but yellow ones do nicely. The seeds are also made into a fairly spicy oil and, of course, into prepared mustards.

Saffron
Zaffran

is sold dried both as yellow-red threads and powdered — expensive in either form, but only a little of this very important spice is needed. Many sweets, rice pillaus and chicken dishes would pine for lack of it.

Salt
Namak

is used in amounts according to personal preference. I can't bear to cook without it.

Turmeric
Haldi

is sold ground and gives a mild flavour and yellow colour to dishes in which it is used, as well as bright yellow stains to skin and cloth, so be careful.

Chillies, red and green
Lal mirch and *hari mirch*

vary in heat and spiciness, the red ones being dried and the fresh ones green. When I find a good variety of whole dried chillies, about 5 cm (2 in) long, I buy a supply and keep them on hand in a jar. Fresh green ones are always to be found in the vegetable drawer of my refrigerator. They vary in size from 5-10 cm (2-4 in), and contain many white seeds, some or all of which you can leave in, if you like spicier food.

Cinnamon
Dar cheeni

comes from the paper-thin bark of a tree, rolled inside one another into sticks. These have so much more flavour than ground cinnamon that I use the sticks whole or broken whenever I want the flavour of cinnamon in my dishes.

Cloves
Long

should be used whole for their superior flavour and splendid fragrance.

Coriander
Dhania

is one of my very favourite spices. Fresh coriander is now sold at many greengrocers. The wonderful flavour and aroma of the fresh green leaves are added towards the end of cooking in many dishes. More familiar is ground coriander, though in my opinion it is better to grind the coriander seeds yourself, or best of all use fresh coriander leaves.

Cumin
Zeera

is used whole and ground. As with coriander seeds, for flavour and fragrance it is best to grind whole cumin seeds into powder just before you use them. I use an electric coffee mill for this purpose and keep another one for grinding coffee.

A note on titles

There are a number of dishes in the book for which the Indian names appear very Westernized. This is because there are no equivalent names for these in Hindi or Urdu. Some of the words, like 'cutlets', 'patties', 'omelettes' and 'chops' are used in daily cooking, but their spelling and pronunciation are completely Indianized. 'Cutlet' would be written and pronounced as *cutless*, omelette as *aam-late*, patties at *paytees* and mutton chop as *mutton chap*. Even in a small town restaurant in India the menu refers to *aam-late*, *paytees* and *cutless*. Of course the recipes are more exotic and the use of spices is heavy, but the words themselves have been borrowed from English in the long association with the British in India.

Some friends comment...

Fast family food

One — hopefully — chooses to remember the parental table in loving detail, recalling long-gone meals, particular dishes that seem never to taste as good anywhere else. 'Mother had some secret ingredient,' one says, or perhaps it was Father, if he lent a hand. One goes out into the world with these memories and in time Mother and Father disappear and someone else takes over cooking for you, or you learn to do it for yourself and, if you do not lead too rootless an existence, the old memories out of the kitchens of childhood are overlaid with new ones. This has happened to me, and now my family table is presided over by Ismail, so that as I approach my second childhood it is the tastes and aromas of *his* food that overwhelmingly colour my memories of eating at home. When I do not get his cooking for a while due to separation or to being on the road with some film, I crave it. It has now become a part of me, if not in the actual physical sense (though it could well be that, too), then certainly overwhelmingly in my perception of what is good in life.

When I first knew Ismail in New York in 1961, had in fact just met him, it was decided to throw a little party in my walk-up apartment on East 62nd Street and to invite the friends we knew mutually, most of whom were Indian, for dinner, where I would screen a (very) rough cut of the documentary I was working on that later became *The Delhi Way*. And it was the usual somewhat alarming situation, with guests arriving and no activity in the kitchen, not even a brown paper bag or two from Gristedes, expensively and reassuringly lop-sided and crammed-looking. What there was was a mess of *pakoras* and *samosas*, quite cold, quite greasy, that had been brought in from a somewhat forlorn Indian restaurant — one of two in the city then — in the Times

12

Square area called The Kashmir, which was the regular haunt of Saeed Jaffrey in those days. He had also been invited to our party. I say 'our', but who do I mean? It was supposed to be *my* party, and I have never had to give one since, because Ismail just takes over, grand Indian host that he is. Chilled wine bottles appear out of the sky, *qeema, dal* and rice are suddenly in evidence (or even better things) as the catered hors d'oeuvres from the Kashmir restaurant are given out, and everyone is happy. So it was that night, so it is every night whether there are guests or not, if we happen to be in the same country: the fast family food, some of it rough and ready, some of it leftover, some of it of a surpassing freshness and delicacy of ingredient and inspiration. This is what I know, this is what I remember.

James Ivory
Film director, who has directed most of the films I have produced.

Working on recipes

Ever since we met, whenever the opportunity arose, I've hung about Ismail's kitchen, a gourmet-chef-groupie. Groupies can be supportive and, I hope, good company at times, but we can also be troublesome. For example, we like to ask questions about what's going on. Not that Ismail doesn't like sharing his knowledge, on the contrary, he loves it. It's just that he cooks very quickly and there is little time for both concentrating on cooking and explaining what he is doing.

Questions can interrupt his flow, but occasionally I have broken through. 'What was that?'
'What?'
'What you just put in?'
'That was black cardamom.'
'How many?'
'Well, that was ... seven ... pods.'

Being an inspirational cook, Ismail is not one to quibble over small amounts of ingredients when he's making a favourite dish. Peering over his shoulder, many have been impressed with his speed, his confidence, his command of his tools, his knowledge of ingredients and, most importantly for me, his fun in cooking.

He has great joy in preparing something wonderful, especially when he serves it to others. He loves to please people and has a great time doing it.

Ismail has taught me to cook and I feel I can manage now quite well. I believe that anyone can by following his recipes, approaching them with the same spirit in which they were created. They will also discover the pleasure and satisfaction that comes from making something delicious for someone else.

Once, feeling very bold, I asked, 'Ismail, can you remember ever making a mistake in the kitchen?' With a look of bewilderment he answered, 'Of course not'.

Could this really be so, I thought? And I considered the number of pots with rice burnt on the bottom that I have scrubbed clean. But to Ismail, burning rice is not a 'mistake'; it is not important at all. It's rather like dropping a spoon; such things happen sometimes. The only real mistake would be in not trying to please one's guests, and he has never failed to try to please them. He tries with all his heart, because he enjoys it so, and because he enjoys it so, he tries with all his heart.

Richard Robbins
Musician, composer/musical director for all my films since The Europeans. *He has also made a documentary of his own,* Sweet Sounds.

Dining with Ismail

Dining with Ismail is always an adventure. If you dine at his home you know you will be well-fed. If he invites you to dine out, the chances are that he has accepted an invitation to dinner and is taking you along as an unexpected guest. So, if you give a dinner party and invite Ismail, you had better prepare for the odd extra guest or two. Better still, ask Ismail to cook for you. I always do.

When I moved back to London in the early 70s, my fourth floor walk-up flat at 82 Cornwall Gardens became Ismail's home in London. As I had just moved in I had no furniture except beds, a couple of carpets and an ancient octagonal dining table I had bought with five uncomfortable rickety chairs from the owners of 'Beechwood', the house outside New York City where we filmed *Savages*. In my living room I placed four unmatched upright chairs in front of a monster TV set which I had got so that we and twenty friends could watch the first broadcast of our film, *Autobiography of a Princess*, at home. This strange collection of uncomfortable furniture did not deter Ismail from having people over for meals.

One morning Ismail announced that he had invited Ingrid Bergman to tea next day and that the four chairs in the living room would not do. I was delighted at the prospect of meeting Miss Bergman, so I went straight out and hurriedly bought a rather odd-looking pair of sofas, to be delivered immediately — but it wasn't soon enough. Ismail, not knowing of my purchase and thinking that Miss Bergman deserved better than the four flights of steep stairs and the discomfort of my flat, had changed his mind and invited her to take tea with him at Claridges instead. And that, to my regret, was how Miss Bergman never sat on my new sofas.

But many friends did make it up all those stairs and were rewarded by heavenly smells of exotic foods and delicious meals. Although it is difficult to pick one evening from the many when unusual and adventurous meals — for English palates — were proudly produced, there was an occasion I do remember as being remarkable. This time, in addition to Jim Ivory, Ismail and me, there was Ruth Jhabvala, a visiting film mogul and his wife. As Ismail handed round unusually strong drinks, he quietly asked me, 'Where's the fish?'

'What fish?' I countered.

'Didn't you get the fish and the broccoli and ...?'

'No, I thought you said you would,' I stammered.

'Do we have any food at all?' Ismail's voice was getting louder.

'Absolutely nothing,' I whispered in a panic. 'I'll dash out!'

'First let's look in the refrigerator,' said Ismail, comparatively calm.

We went to look: a few eggs, five sprigs of tired parsley, half a carton of yoghurt, some cooked rice, two wrinkled lemons, last night's cold string beans, and in the freezer, half a package of pitta bread. All in all, it was a small assortment of odds and ends. Ismail looked serious. 'I'll see what I can do,' he said, like a surgeon facing a particularly difficult operation. Only too willingly I left him to it.

Fourteen minutes later, Ismail blithely emerged from the kitchen bearing a tray laden with a spectacular egg curry with rice, raita, dal, potatoes, onions, string beans in lemon butter, hot pitta bread, and his mother's famous green mango chutney from Bombay. A feast fit for a mogul. If I had not witnessed this miracle of speed and culinary alchemy I would have assumed that Ismail had been planning the menu for days. I think that even Ingrid Bergman would happily have put up with the steep stairs and a hard chair for this meal.

Anthony Korner
Publisher of Art Forum, *also occasional film-maker who has collaborated with me on* Savages, Helen, *and* Autobiography of a Princess.

The producer as Foodie

To know Ismail is to eat with him — or, more likely, to be fed by him. He knows that the way to an actor's art is through his stomach, and he shamelessly deploys this knowledge to obtain your services, your quiescence, your goodwill. The phrase 'to curry favour' was probably invented with Ismail in mind.

And what curries! We had already known each other for some years before I supped at his table. This was a mere oversight on Ismail's part, or, rather, a lapse of memory which I was too shy to correct.

'You remember that wonderful dinner I gave in Paris that you gatecrashed with Peggy Ramsay?' I didn't, for several good reasons. Peggy and I had not been in Paris at the same time, I had just slipped fleetingly onto the set of *Quartet*, and would rather have died than gatecrash a group of people who knew each other but not me. 'Yes,' I nonetheless lied, because it seemed so much easier, and somehow less disappointing, 'yes, what a marvellous meal that was!' So whenever Ismail and I bumped into each other, he would jovially recall the now legendary meal, and the memory of it would grow rosier and rosier.

One evening we went to see a play of shattering ponderousness, and as we joyously fled at the interval, Ismail (to whom an evening without a meal would be an offence against nature) steered us swiftly towards the excellent Vietnamese restaurant in

Frith Street. As we awaited our dishes, he started to regale our fellow diners with the mythic meal, and with my breathtaking audacity in the gatecrashing department. Suddenly he broke all the rules and asked me, 'What was it we had that evening? I don't remember.'

'Well,' I paused, 'uh, curry?'

'Yes, yes, of course there was curry, but what *kind* of curry?' My experience of Indian food was at that time limited to fairly bitter memories of late-night poppadoms in provincial towns, so I gawped somewhat.

'Er, wasn't it, er, snail curry, I thought, with capers, and um, chestnuts,' thinking, France and he probably used all the local stuff.

A smile of apparent recollection spread over his face. 'Of course,' he said, 'what a wonderful memory you have, even for ingredients. Wonderful!'

Since then I have had many marvellous curries with Ismail, none better than those on the set of *A Room With A View* in Florence. It is, however, agonizing to watch the poor man torn between being a host and being a producer. He is passionately eager that you should consume his magical concoctions, as much and as late as you like, and equally passionate that you should appear on the set next morning fresh, on time and not too fat.

'Eat!' he cries, 'but quickly! And not too much! But have you had any of this? You must, I insist! I've called you a cab, you can have another helping of dal while you wait. Take it with you! Yes, yes, but *go*, I implore you.'

Simon Callow
Well-known English actor and writer, whom I had long wanted to cast in one of my films and at last succeeded with A Room With A View.

Friend's observation

England breeds an organized and generally rather prescribed way of living. I escaped from this when I lived for two years in Italy, where spontaneity and last minute feasts are the order of the day. However, that was sixteen years ago, and when Ismail and I plotted a jointly hosted, Merchant cuisine evening at my flat in the Albany, I set about the preparations with the customary advanced planning. Six guests were invited by Ismail and five by me. It was to be a gourmet evening and an occasion when Marion Donaldson, his editor at Futura, could sample Ismail's skills. Among the many people who know him, Ismail's reputation in the kitchen is already a legend.

The arrangement was that apart from providing the setting I would prepare some basic ingredients. At the 'pre-arranged' hour of 7.15-7.30 Ismail was due to appear with his ingredients. By 8.00, no Ismail and unknown guests due to appear any minute. At 8.10 the bell tore through my nervousness and with trepidation I opened the door: Ismail, adorned with overflowing plastic bags and a rare and beautiful Kashmir shawl, rolled in wreathed in smiles. And so to cook.

By 8.45 the assembled guests were smiling, tantalized by the delicate aromas wafting about the rooms. Old friends such as Madhur Jaffrey, Terence Stamp, Ravi and Caroline Misra and Raimond Buitons could fantasize with some authenticity on the work of the thirty-five-minute magician in the kitchen. Uninitiated, Anthony Smith of the British Film Institute, Edward Adeane of Palaces Royal and Nicole Mackey of Rank Films could imagine less precisely what elusive surprises were in store. By playing cook's assistant for twenty to thirty minutes, I had hoped to cull some secrets, but Ismail's nimble fingers and improvisations were too quick, so even for me each dish had its own delicate surprise.

Since that meal, when I invite close friends to dinner, they very often ask me whether or not Ismail will be cooking. There is a distinct note of disappointment on those occasions when I say no. I have even overheard some of these same close friends offering freshly caught trout to Ismail — not to me — for our next 'joint' Albany dinner!

Sarah Fox-Pitt
Curator of Contemporary Arts at the Tate Gallery, and a contributor to various periodicals on contemporary art.

My idea of giving the perfect dinner party: Ismail cooks

Out of the blue, during the summer of '84, Ismail phoned to say he was in town. 'Let's meet at your place for dinner, let's all meet,' he enthused, as dinner for Ismail always seems to include as many people as possible.

'Oh, Ismail,' I wailed, 'I'm in rehearsal all day and won't be home until at least six thirty. There's no food in the fridge,' and similar lame excuses.

'Don't worry,' he said. 'I'll cook!'

I got back from work tired and dusty, leapt in and out of the bath, fluffed a few cushions and put out some peanuts. At 6.45, I opened my door to a beaming Ismail bearing four bulging carrier bags containing what would be dinner for the masses — surely he had invited many more by now.

For the twenty or more years I've known him, Ismail has always managed, remarkably, to fit in shopping for beautiful food in between meetings and filming. In the old days when we were all younger and poorer, Ismail would turn up with even the salt and pepper and the odd pound of butter just in case we didn't have any in stock. This evening he had bought fresh fish, mushrooms, bread, garlic, fresh herbs and spices, green beans, salad ingredients and the rice he's so fond of, *basmati*. He made himself at home in the kitchen with a glass of cold white wine and with great panache set to, flourishing a knife, chopping garlic and onions. He has a genius for walking into a kitchen, any kitchen, bustling about for half an hour and producing a feast fit for the gods, never having to ask where the oil is kept or anything so mundane as that.

The guests arrived, mostly family and close friends. We sat looking at the rose garden, watching the Thames and sipping our wine, while smells of fabulous food came from the kitchen. In twenty minutes Ismail had everything under control and joined us. That evening we were a particularly happy group of people. Ismail was in town with Jim Ivory and Dick Robbins was with them. Also with us were my sister Jennifer, her daughter Sanjana and Michael, my husband.

The meal was a triumph and, as always, there was a fight over the last green bean and the last magnificent mushrooms. Eating Ismail's food causes people to forget their usual manners when it comes to the last available bites. That evening was typical of the many meals we have shared together in different houses and in different countries. It ended with a walk in the garden, coffee, chocolates and a lot of laughs. There was a feeling of happy togetherness, with no hassles, the hostess having done nothing but provide the kitchen and a few pots and pans. It was a magical occasion, like many in the past and, I hope, many to come and all because Ismail said, 'I'll cook!'

Felicity Kendal ...
whose very first starring role, I'm proud to say, was in Shakespeare-Wallah.

'Guess who's coming to dinner'

'Who? Ingrid Bergman? Ismail, are you serious!' My mind didn't race, it began to shriek. What should I cook? Who else should come? Oh God, you mean *here* this evening!? I began to rage, 'Ismail, you are joking. How can I be expected to prepare?' I tailed off as Ismail's warm, soothing, Bombay-clad voice gently eased me back to earth.

'Ruth and Ava Jhabvala are also coming and Ingrid's agent Kay Brown, a wonderful New Yorker — and of course I'll be there,' as if that would solve everything. 'At eight, then. I'll do the cooking, so go and get ...' he continued, giving me a surprisingly short list of ingredients, nothing extraordinary — pretty simple, really.

I spent all day rehearsing: 'How do you do, Miss Bergman.' No, too formal. 'Hi, Ingrid, welcome to the Korners.' No, too informal. And deciding what to wear: finery and formal or free and freaky. And nervous about meeting this high-powered agent from New York; she sounded formidable. Oh, if only I had read English Literature at least.

The day raced past. The ingredients were bought and laid out and chores were all done.

Six thirty passed: no Ismail. Seven p.m.: nerves stretched to breaking point and still no Ismail. At 7.05 the phone rang. 'Ismail, where are you?' Soothing excuses didn't work this time. 'Get over here,' I said with venom.

He arrived cool as the Indian Guru from *Bombay Talkie*. The chickens were stuffed with mushrooms, ginger and parsley. Lemon juice was squeezed over them and the squeezed peel stuffed inside, mustard was painted over and the birds thrown in the oven. The peas were organized and rice put in pots, everything done in ten minutes. Ismail suggested we go upstairs and have a drink and I weakly asked, 'That's all?'

Ingrid and Kay arrived punctually at eight, Kay carrying her own bottle of whisky, 'knowing Ismail well,' she explained. The evening was marvellous, the food Ismailishly delicious and Kay and the lovely Ingrid were star guests.

Sandra Korner
Aficionado of my cooking and my films.

Hors d'oeuvres and drinks

Here I include some recipes for drinks (alcoholic and non-alcoholic) and for some Indian-inspired hors d'oeuvres.

With regard to alcohol, I generally do not serve much more than white wine or cold beer when I invite guests. Over the years, my friends who wanted whiskey often had to bring their own bottle. When I remember to have it around, I do, otherwise I don't worry. It seems to me that spirits dull all the senses, and I want the taste buds to remain fully receptive to what I have in store for them. Even so, I admit that on a hot summer day, a gin and tonic can be a delight. ...

Mustard and chive prawn bites

Rai aur piyaz chingri chat

This is an hors d'oeuvre I concocted for two of my food and cookery-loving friends, Jeannie and Allen Miller.

Preparation and cooking time: about 20 minutes   *Serves 6–8*

900g/2lb raw prawns, defrosted if frozen
3 bay leaves, crumbled
salt
3 tablespoons snipped chives, or 1 tablespoon freeze-dried chives
2 tablespoons Dijon mustard
¼ teaspoon cayenne pepper
4 tablespoons lemon juice

Shell and clean the prawns.

Heat a saucepan of water with the bay leaves to the boil. Salt it generously and add the prawns. Cook for 1–1½ minutes, drain, then refresh them immediately in cold running water. Drain well and pat the prawns dry on kitchen paper.

Mix the chives, mustard, cayenne pepper and lemon juice together.

Stir the mixture into the well-drained prawns and serve skewered on cocktail sticks.

Deep-fried Cheddar balls

Paneer bhajya

Preparation and cooking time: about 25 minutes   *Serves 6–8*

225 g/8 oz Cheddar cheese, finely grated
2 large eggs
2 tablespoons chick pea (gram) flour
¼ teaspooon baking powder
1 green chilli, seeded (optional) and chopped
2 teaspoons chopped coriander leaves
¼ teaspoon salt
vegetable oil for deep frying
tomato chutney, to serve

Mix the cheese, eggs, flour, baking powder, chilli, coriander leaves and salt thoroughly. If the mixture is too wet, add in a little more flour; if it is too dry, mix in a little more beaten egg white.

Form the mixture into teaspoonfuls and put them aside on a dish.

Heat the oil in a deep-fat frier, or in a saucepan to a depth of about 5 cm/2 in until it is quite hot. Carefully transfer the cheese balls to the hot oil and cook, in batches if necessary, until they are golden.

Drain the balls on kitchen paper and serve them hot and skewered on cocktail sticks; good with Tomato chutney (page 220).

Bombay vegetable fritters
Bambai bhajya

Preparation and cooking time: *Serves 6–8*
*   letting the batter rest 30 minutes, plus about 30 minutes*

1 small cauliflower, cut into bite-sized florets
2 medium-sized onions, thickly sliced and divided into rings
2–3 medium-sized potatoes, boiled until just tender, then cooled under
*   cold running water, drained, peeled and cut into bite-sized rounds*
vegetable oil for deep frying
For the batter
2 teaspoons vegetable oil
175g/6oz chick pea (gram) flour
1½ teaspoons salt
1 teaspoon ground cumin
1 teaspoon ground coriander
½ teaspoon cayenne pepper

First make the batter. Rub the oil into the flour until the oil is evenly absorbed. Mix in the salt, cumin, coriander and cayenne pepper.

Slowly pour in 225ml/8floz warm water, beating continuously until the mixture is thin and smooth. A food processor or electric blender does this admirably.

Let the batter stand for about 30 minutes. Meanwhile prepare the vegetables.

Heat the oil in a deep-fat frier or in a large saucepan to a depth of about 5cm/2in. When it is quite hot, dip the vegetables into the batter, shaking off the excess, and fry them in batches until they turn golden brown.

Drain them on kitchen paper and serve them hot, with cocktail sticks.

Fresh sardine snacks

Taze sardine ki chat

Preparation and cooking time:　　　　　　　　　*Serves 6–8*
　1–2 hours marinating, plus 20 minutes

juice of 2 lemons
4 tablespoons Dijon mustard
1 teaspoon dried tarragon
450g/1 lb fresh sardines, cleaned
vegetable oil for frying

Whisk the lemon juice, mustard and tarragon together.

Lay the sardines in one layer in a non-metal dish and pour over the lemon juice mixture. Leave the sardines to marinate for 1–2 hours, turning them in the marinade occasionally.

Heat oil to a depth of about 12mm/½in in a frying-pan over medium-low heat. When hot, shake the excess marinade from the sardines and transfer them carefully to the oil. Reduce the heat, partially cover and fry the fish gently for 10–15 minutes, turning them occasionally.

Drain the sardines on kitchen paper and serve them warm or at room temperature with cocktail sticks for skewering.

Sweet lassi
Meethi lassi

Preparation and cooking time: *Serves 6*
    10 minutes, plus chilling (optional)

850 ml/1½ pt plain yoghurt
125 ml/4 fl oz rosewater
4 tablespoons sugar
1 dozen shelled, unsalted pistachios, coarsely chopped

Whisk all the ingredients with 850 ml/1½ pt water for 3–4 minutes until the mixture becomes frothy.

Serve at room temperature or chilled.

Salty lassi
Namkeen lassi

Preparation and cooking time: *Serves 6*
    10 minutes, plus chilling (optional)

850 ml/1½ pt plain yoghurt
½ teaspoon salt
½ teaspoon ground cumin

Whisk together all the ingredients with 850 ml/1½ pt water for 3–4 minutes until the mixture becomes frothy. Correct the seasoning and serve at room temperature or chilled.

A better gin and tonic

Preparation time: 5 minutes   *Serves 1*

ice cubes
50 ml/2 fl oz superior dry gin
freshly squeezed juice of ½ lemon or lime
tonic water
slice of lemon or lime to garnish

Fill a tall glass with ice cubes and add the gin.

Add the lemon or lime juice and fill the glass with tonic water.
Add the lemon or lime slice, and serve.

Vodka with soda or tonic and mint

I suggest that this be enjoyed in a hammock. Do not try to navigate after drinking.

Preparation time: 5 minutes   *Serves 1*

ice cubes
50 ml/2 fl oz 100 proof vodka
8–10 fresh mint leaves
soda or tonic water

Fill a large wine goblet with ice cubes and add the vodka.

Add the mint leaves, stir them vigorously, fill the glass with soda or tonic water and serve.

Beer and lemon for a hot afternoon

This is a very satisfying drink for a sultry day.

Preparation time: 5 minutes   *Serves 1*

ice cubes
275 ml/10 fl oz lager
freshly squeezed juice of ½ lemon
sprig of mint, to garnish

Fill a tall glass with ice, then add the lager.
Stir in the lemon juice, insert the mint and serve.

Soups

J ames Ivory, the director and my collaborator for many years, is a soup specialist who has inspired several of these soup recipes. He makes really exceptional soups, and goes about making them with great care, cutting and chopping so that the ingredients all look just right. I, on the other hand, am far more casual about the appearance of my soups, briskly chopping away with far less attention to detail. We may make films but not soup together, for collaboration is not good when making a soup. A soup should be the result of one cook, and one cook alone, as the saying goes, so try not to collaborate. There is rarely ever agreement about the right amount of salt, for example, when two parties season the cooking soup.

One of my favourite lunches — any time of the year — is a really terrific soup, an exceptional salad, and very fresh bread, served hot, and a glass of good wine or beer. It is a superb menu for anybody. My soups are both hearty and spicy, with an Indian touch I hope you will enjoy.

Broccoli and lemon gazpacho

Broccoli aur nimboo ka sorba

This is one of the recipes being discussed during the dinner party in my film *Jane Austen in Manhattan,* when Anne Baxter's pearls fall into the soup.

Preparation and cooking time: 40 minutes, plus chilling   Serves 6

350g/12oz fresh tender broccoli tops, cut into bite-sized florets (about 700g/1½lb broccoli stalks)
25g/1oz butter
1 large onion, peeled and chopped
1.4L/2½pt chicken stock
rind of ½ lemon
juice of ½ lemon
10 large garlic cloves, peeled and chopped
425ml/15floz single cream
salt

Reserve a few of the broccoli florets for a garnish and lightly steam the rest of the florets. Do not overcook, in order to retain colour and crispness. Remove the florets from the pan and let them cool.

Melt the butter in a large saucepan over medium-low heat, add the onion and cook until it begins to brown, stirring occasionally.

Add the broccoli, stock, lemon rind and juice to the pan. Raise the heat until the soup barely simmers, turn the heat to low, cover and cook 15 minutes or until the lemon is soft.

Put the soup, in stages, through a food processor or blender, along with the uncooked garlic. Add the cream and salt to taste. Cool and chill the soup.

Garnish the soup with the reserved broccoli florets to serve.

Indian gazpacho

Hindustani gazpacho

One can make gazpacho out of all sorts of things. Virtually any raw vegetables will do, provided they have some crispness. Here is a very tangy version that requires no cooking.

Preparation and cooking time: 20 minutes, plus chilling   Serves 6

6 large tomatoes, blanched and skinned
1 large onion, preferably red
1 large green or red pepper
2 bunches of radishes, trimmed
3 large carrots
3 large celery sticks
2 medium-sized cucumbers, unpeeled
2 hot green chillies, seeded (optional)
6–8 large garlic cloves, peeled
2 tablespoons olive oil
75–125 g/3–4 oz tomato purée
1.4 L/2½ pt chicken stock
425 ml/15 fl oz dry red wine
salt

Chop all the vegetables and mix them in a large container with the chillies, garlic, olive oil, tomato purée, chicken stock and red wine.

Put the mixture, in stages, through a food processor or blender. Do not let the soup become too thin; make sure there are no chunks of unprocessed vegetables. Add salt to taste and chill before serving.

Ginger broccoli soup

Adrak broccoli walla shorba

Preparation and cooking time: 25 minutes   *Serves 4*

15 g/½ oz butter
1 medium-sized onion, halved and finely sliced
850 ml/1½ pt chicken stock
575 ml/1 pt water
25 mm/1 in fresh ginger root, grated
½ teaspoon cayenne pepper
juice of 1 lemon
175 g/6 oz fresh tender broccoli tops, cut into bite-sized florets (about
  350 g/12 oz broccoli stalks)

Melt the butter in a saucepan over medium-low heat, add the onion and cook until it begins to brown, stirring occasionally.

Meanwhile, heat the stock, water and grated ginger in a saucepan for 5–6 minutes. Do not boil.

Add the onions, cayenne pepper, lemon juice, and then the broccoli to the liquid. Cook over medium heat, stirring occasionally, for 7 more minutes. Do not let the soup boil. Serve right away.

Hot rough tomato soup

Tez tamatar shorba

You can add pasta to this soup towards the end of cooking. I suggest 2 tablespoons of pastina, tiny specks of pasta that can be added to the soup for 10 minutes before serving.

Preparation and cooking time: about 1¼ hours   *Serves 6*

3 large or 6 medium-sized ripe tomatoes
2 tablespoons butter
1 large onion, peeled and coarsely chopped
1 small potato, diced small
175 g/6 oz tomato purée
2 L/3 pt chicken stock
pinch of thyme
2 small dried chillies, seeded (optional) and chopped
6 cloves
12 peppercorns
3 bay leaves, crumbled
salt

Drop the tomatoes in boiling water to cover and remove the pan from the heat. After 1 minute, remove each tomato in turn and peel away the skin. Cut the tomatoes into rough chunks.

Melt the butter in a large saucepan over medium-low heat, add onions and cook until it begins to turn golden, stirring frequently and reducing the heat if necessary.

Add the tomatoes to the onions with the potato, tomato purée, chicken stock, thyme, chillies, cloves, peppercorns, bay leaves and salt to taste.

Simmer the mixture gently for 45 minutes to 1 hour.

Claverack carrot soup

Claverack ka khas gajar shorba

This is a variation on potage Crécy.

Preparation and cooking time: about 1 hour   *Serves 4–6*

50g/2oz unsalted butter
450g/1lb carrots, peeled and thinly sliced
1 large onion, peeled and chopped
2 large potatoes, peeled and coarsely diced
5cm/2in fresh ginger root, peeled and grated
850ml/1½pt chicken stock
salt
275ml/10floz single cream

Melt half the butter in a small pan over low heat, add the carrots, stir, cover and cook until they soften, stirring occasionally.

Meanwhile, melt the rest of the butter in a large saucepan over low heat, add the onion and cook until it is soft, stirring occasionally. Remove the pan from the heat.

Add the carrots with the pan juices to the onions with the potatoes, ginger and chicken stock. Bring the mixture to a boil, reduce the heat and simmer for 30 minutes.

Add salt to taste. If the soup is too thick add a little water or stock. Stir the cream into the hot soup and serve.

*   As the ginger creates a tangy flavour like pepper, pepper is not necessary. For those who particularly like ginger, double the amount.

Avocado and tomato soup
Avocado aur tamatar ka sorba

Preparation and cooking time: 15 minutes, plus chilling   *Serves 2–3*

3 medium-sized ripe avocados
275 ml/10 floz vegetable or chicken stock
125 ml/4 floz cream
1–2 teaspoons grated, strained onion juice
125 ml/4 floz tomato purée
1½ teaspoons lemon juice, or to taste
salt and pepper

Remove the seeds and skin from the avocados. Mash the flesh in a large bowl.

Whisk in the stock, cream, onion juice, tomato purée and lemon juice.

Season with salt and pepper, and more lemon juice, if wished, and chill before serving.

* If you eliminate the tomato purée you will have a paler and milder-tasting soup, but the flavour of the avocados will become more prominent.

Hearty soup

Dilkhush shorba

What makes this soup distinctive is the ginger and dill, though the other ingredients, both fresh and leftover, may be varied according to what is found in the refrigerator. For example, chicken or sausage may be substituted for beef.

Preparation and cooking time: 35 minutes   *Serves 4–6*

2 tablespoons butter
3 medium-sized carrots, thinly sliced
2 small onions, peeled and chopped
4 × 400 ml/14 oz canned beef consommé, or
1.4 L/2½ pt beef or chicken stock
175–225 g/6–8 oz boneless roast beef, finely diced
1 large potato, diced small
25 mm/1 in fresh ginger root, grated
2 tablespoons chopped fresh dill, or 2 teaspoons dill weed
1 medium-sized red pepper, sliced into slender pieces
6 garlic cloves, peeled and chopped
pinch of chilli powder
½ teaspoon salt

Melt the butter in a large saucepan over medium-low heat, add the onions and carrots and cook until the onions begin to brown, stirring occasionally.

Add the consommé or stock to the pan with the meat, potato, ginger, dill, half the pepper, garlic, chilli powder and salt. Bring the liquid to a boil, then reduce the heat and simmer gently for 20–25 minutes or until the potatoes are very tender.

Correct the seasoning, stir in the rest of the pepper slices and serve.

Sorrel soup

Soral shorba

My friend Joanna Rose visits me in Claverack, New York, and we spend time together there in my vegetable and herb garden discussing and debating the merits of each plant. She is very knowledgeable about many things, and also a good cook. She suggested this recipe for sorrel soup.

Preparation and cooking time: *Serves 4*
    preparing the sorrel, plus 30 minutes

2 tablespoons butter
175g/6oz sorrel leaves, trimmed and washed
1.1L/2pt chicken stock
25g/1oz fresh or frozen, defrosted green peas, puréed
3 egg yolks
125ml/4floz single cream
4 tablespoons chopped fresh chervil or 1 tablespoon dried chervil

Melt the butter in a saucepan over low heat. Add the sorrel and cook 4–5 minutes or until the leaves wilt, stirring occasionally.

Remove the pan from the heat, add the chicken stock and pea purée and put the pan over medium heat.

When the liquid is hot but not too close to boiling, remove it from the heat. Beat the egg yolks into the cream and stir them into the soup.

Put the pan over medium-low heat and stir gently until the soup thickens slightly, but do not let it boil. Sprinkle chervil over the top and serve.

* To serve cold, stir in 150ml/5floz soured cream instead of the pea purée, cream and egg yolks.

Red lentil soup

Masoor dal shorba

Preparation and cooking time: about 30 minutes   *Serves 6*

3 tablespoons vegetable oil
1 medium-sized onion, peeled and chopped
12 peppercorns
4 bay leaves, crumbled
850 ml/1½ pt chicken stock
225 g/8 oz masoor dal (split red lentils), picked over, washed and
    drained
2 tablespoons chopped fresh parsley
3 dry red chillies, seeded (optional)
¼–½ in piece of fresh ginger root, grated

Heat the oil in a large saucepan over low heat. Add the onion and cook until it begins to soften, about 5 minutes, stirring occasionally.

Add the peppercorns and bay leaves and cook a further 5 minutes.

Add the chicken stock, 225 g/8 oz water, the drained red lentils, parsley, chillies and salt to taste. Cook over medium heat, stirring occasionally, for 10 minutes.

When the soup begins to boil, add the grated ginger. Continue cooking for another 10 minutes or until the lentils are very soft and serve.

Potato watercress soup

Aloo aur hari pati ka shorba

Preparation and cooking time: about 1¼ hours   *Serves 6*

4 large potatoes
50g/2oz butter
2 medium-sized onions, peeled and chopped
850ml/1½pt chicken stock
4 large garlic cloves, peeled and chopped
1–1½ teaspoons freshly ground white pepper
1 bunch of watercress, stems removed
salt
575ml/1pt milk

Boil the potatoes in a saucepan until very tender, with the skins on or off, as you prefer, 15–20 minutes. The skins are healthy and good, and the soup will look agreeably speckled if you leave them on. Drain the potatoes.

Meanwhile, melt the butter in a large saucepan over low heat. Add the onions and cook until they soften but do not colour, 8–10 minutes. Remove from the heat.

Add the chicken stock to the onions with the garlic, potatoes and pepper. Bring to a simmer and cook for 25 minutes.

Sprinkle the watercress on top of the simmering liquid, do not mix in, and continue cooking for another 5 minutes.

Purée the mixture in a food processor or blender, in stages if necessary. Season with salt. Return the mixture to the saucepan.

Add the milk to the potato mixture. Heat the soup until it is very hot but does not boil, then serve.

* To serve this soup cold, simply stir the milk into the puréed mixture, cool and chill. Serve the soup garnished with fresh watercress leaves or with about 3 peeled thinly sliced garlic cloves scattered over the top.

Fresh mushroom soup

Taza kumbhi ka shorba

Here is a very rich, delicious soup, but it is so filling that it might be unwise to begin a heavy meal with it. The soup is rather Middle-European in style, and one might ask what it's doing in this cookbook, but I concocted it with local ingredients, in my kitchen in Claverack, New York.

Preparation and cooking time: about 1 hour   *Serves 6*

50–75g/2–3oz butter
1 large onion, peeled and chopped
450g/1lb button mushrooms, washed and sliced
275ml/10floz dry red or white wine (I prefer red)
850ml/1½pt chicken stock
425ml/15floz double cream
small bunch of fresh parsley, finely chopped

Melt 25g/1oz of the butter in a small frying-pan over medium-low heat, add the onion and cook 2–3 minutes, stirring frequently. It should not become too soft. Remove from the heat.

Heat another 25g/1oz butter in a large saucepan over medium-low heat, add the mushrooms and cook them 8–10 minutes, adding more butter as needed.

When the mushrooms are soft, add the wine and cook the mushrooms for 5 more minutes.

Add the chicken stock and onion to the mushrooms and simmer gently for 15 minutes over a low flame. Do not let the mixture boil.

Coarsely purée the mixture in batches in a food processor or blender.

When ready to serve, reheat the mushroom mixture, turn the heat to low and stir in the cream. When hot but not boiling, serve the soup garnished with a sprinkling of parsley.

White gazpacho soup

Safaid gazpacho shorba

My friend Phyllis Parker gave me this recipe and I am proud to share it with you.

Preparation and cooking time: Serves 6–8
    about 1 hour, plus cooling if wished

about 25 g/1 oz butter
1 large onion, peeled and chopped
2 large cucumbers, peeled and thinly sliced
1.4 L/2½ pt chicken stock
the leaves of 3–4 fresh mint sprigs, plus extra to garnish, optional
4 tablespoons ground almonds
425 ml/15 fl oz single cream
salt

Melt 25 g/1 oz butter in a frying-pan over medium-low heat, add the onion and cook until it just begins to brown, stirring frequently.

Add the cucumbers to the pan and cook over low heat for 2–3 minutes, stirring frequently. Do not let them brown. Add more butter if necessary.

Put the chicken stock, onion and cucumber in a large saucepan, heat to a simmer, then reduce the heat to low, cover and cook for 20 minutes.

Add the mint to the mixture and put it through a food processor or blender.

Whisk the ground almonds and cream into the mixture. Season with salt.

Reheat but do not boil the soup, or cool and chill and serve it as a cold soup. If the latter, reserve some small sprigs of mint as a garnish.

Fish

Bombay, the capital of the state of Maharashtra, India, is a great port, so there is a great deal of fishing in the area. My father and I would regularly go to Nul Bazaar to buy fish. This section of the market had fish stalls with marble slabs and wicker baskets underneath. The marble slabs would rest on the wicker baskets and the fish, freshly caught by the Maharashtra women, would lie in rows on top of the marble. The fisherwomen were ready to clean and scale the fish, cut it into pieces with their very sharp knives and prepare it for the customer. They argued and gestured, trying to catch the attention of those strolling through the market. There were 100-125 fisherwomen sitting very closely together, with each stall about two steps apart. The women would have pomfrets, striped bass, sea bass, mackerel, prawns, tiny shrimps, fresh 'Bombay Duck' (really a fish), and occasionally lobsters and crabs. I learned to recognize a good fish from a bad fish by pressing the head of the fish near the gills. If the fish is fresh, a white substance will form at the gill openings. If a red liquid forms, the buyer should beware: the fish is not fresh.

At the bazaar there was always great haggling over the prices of fish as there were no signs to tell us what the prices were. Fish were sold singly, in pairs, in fours, or tens or whatever you wanted; but you would always have to haggle with the fisher- women, and great rows would occur with occasional screaming and shouting, just as fishwives are said to do. If you looked shocked at the price they asked for the fish, you could offer them twenty per cent or twenty-five per cent lower. The fisherwomen would then say nasty words to you such as, 'Move on to the next stall! I have fish that only a connoisseur would buy and you are not that person.' This phrase would be said by practically every fisherwoman in the bazaar. 'You are not a connoisseur of fish, and my fish is only for the connoisseur!'

My father knew how to deal with these women. He would ask for a particular fish, usually pomfret, a lovely diamond-shaped fish and a favourite in Bombay. The women would bring out a wonderful pair of pomfrets. My father would never argue, as his reputation was that he would pay the top rupee for good fish, and he was never sold anything which was not the best quality. He was always offered the fish that had just been brought in to the market, because he frequented the stalls of two or three of his favourite fisherwomen. They expected him and would keep their best fish aside for him. Even if someone else came and offered them more money, they would keep the fish for him because of his reputation for buying the best. He actually ended up often paying much less than other customers!

Fish was prepared in our home with lots of coconut and fresh tamarind, which is yellow-green in colour, and dark tamarind, which is brown, almost black, in colour. The dark tamarind gives a sour taste but it is wonderful with pomfret and coconut sauce. With the fish we always had *kichri* (see page 181), a dish made with a particular kind of lentil (*toor dal*) (see page 190) and rice. This fish dinner was served with homemade mango pickle, and with poppadoms baked on charcoal as opposed to a cooker. This would be a great meal in the afternoon, particularly in the monsoon season when an abundance of pomfrets was available in the market.

In my fish recipes there are lots of variations I have tried with mustard, coriander and coconut. I have also combined ingredients such as dried French herbs and lemon with the fish. I have prepared fish baked, grilled, and cooked on top of the stove. I enjoy fish enormously. I think that fish is one of the most healthy things you can eat, and it's also one of the best tasting. I can never understand someone who says, 'I don't like fish'; I think that a person misses half of the enjoyment of food if he can't appreciate fish. Fish roes are also delicious, and I have included a recipe for them in the book.

Curried fish in yoghurt

Dahi-walli machli

Preparation and cooking time: 25 minutes   *Serves 4-6*

275 ml/6 fl oz vegetable oil
700 g/1½ lb boned, skinned turbot, salmon or other firm-fleshed fish,
    cut into large bite-sized pieces
2 large onions, peeled and grated
8 garlic cloves, pressed
4 cm/1½ in fresh ginger root, grated
1 teaspoon cumin seeds
¼ teaspoon turmeric
1 teaspoon chilli powder
225 ml/8 fl oz plain yoghurt
½ teaspoon salt
1 teaspoon sugar
⅛ teaspoon saffron powder

Heat 125 ml/4 fl oz of the oil in the frying-pan over medium heat. When hot, fry the pieces of fish until they are lightly browned on all sides. Drain and reserve them.

Add the rest of the oil to the pan and fry the onions over medium-low heat until they begin to turn golden. Add the garlic, ginger, cumin, turmeric and chilli powder and fry for 2 minutes.

Add the yoghurt, salt, sugar and saffron, bring to the boil, lower the heat and simmer gently for 10 minutes.

Add the fish, cover and cook for 2–3 minutes to heat it through. Serve immediately with Basmati pillau (page 185).

Ismail's spicy fish roe

Masaledar machli ke unde

Preparation and cooking time: 25–30 minutes   *Serves 6*

900 g/2 lb of cod's roe in one piece
¼ teaspoon salt
4 tablespoons vegetable oil
1 teaspoon cumin seeds
1½ teaspoons freshly ground black pepper
3 tablespoons Dijon mustard
125 ml/4 fl oz lemon juice
2 teaspoons fresh dill

Bring a large saucepan of water almost to the boil. Add the roe carefully with the salt, let the water come just to the boil, then lower the heat to a simmer.

When the roe begins to become firm, remove it from the water, draining in a colander.

Place the drained roe in a bowl and mash it well and reserve.

Heat the oil in a frying-pan over medium-low heat. Add the cumin seeds and black pepper and fry them for 30 seconds.

Stir in the mustard, then the roe, lemon juice and dill and cook for 5–10 minutes. Serve warm.

Spicy fried pomfret

Masaledar tale pomfret

Pomfrets are delicious fish from the ocean around Bombay, which are available cleaned and frozen in the West. If they are too large for easy cooking, cut them across in two.

Preparation and cooking time: Serves 2
   15 minutes seasoning the fish, plus 15 minutes

4 pomfrets, each about 20cm/8in long, cleaned and defrosted if frozen
vegetable oil for frying
15g/5oz dried breadcrumbs
For the masala* paste
1 teaspoon chilli powder
½ teaspoon turmeric
4 tablespoons dried parsley flakes or chopped fresh parsley
4 tablespoons vinegar
6 tablespoons Dijon mustard
1 teaspoon freshly ground black pepper
½ teaspoon salt

Mix the ingredients together for the *masala* (spice) paste. Cover the fish with the paste and leave for 15 minutes.

Fill a deep frying-pan with about 25mm/1in of oil and let it heat over a medium heat. Meanwhile coat the fish in the breadcrumbs, shaking off the excess.

When the oil is hot, fry the fish for 8–10 minutes, turning once, in batches if necessary, until the crumbs are nicely browned. Serve right away with crusty French bread and a green salad.

* spice mixture

Mackerel in coconut sauce

Naryal machli ka salan

Preparation and cooking time: *Serves 6*
  making the coconut sauce, plus 20 minutes

2–3 large mackerel or bluefish (about 1.8–2.3 kg/4–5 lb in all),
  cleaned, discarding head and tail
425 ml/15 fl oz spicy coconut sauce (page 52)

Cut the fish into steaks of even thickness.

Add the coconut sauce to a saucepan and bring to the boil.

Add the fish steaks and simmer gently over lowered heat for 5–8 minutes or until done. Serve with plain boiled rice.

Lobster in spicy coconut sauce

Seepdar machli aur naryal ka salan

This is a heavenly dish, worth the trouble and expense, and you can cook up to eight lobster tails in the same amount of sauce by adding a little more hot water with the bay leaves.

Preparation and cooking time: *Serves 4*
   making the coconut sauce, plus 20 minutes

4 tablespoons vegetable oil
1 teaspoon black mustard seeds
4 bay leaves
575 ml/1 pt spicy coconut sauce (page 52)
4 lobster tails

Heat the oil in a large, deep saucepan over medium-low heat, add the mustard seeds and let them cook for 1 minute.

Add the bay leaves and coconut sauce and simmer over medium heat for 5 minutes.

Add the lobster tails, and simmer gently for 5 minutes or until the flesh is firm but not overcooked. If bought already cooked, just heat them through.

Serve the lobster with Basmati pillau (page 185) or Saffron pillau (page 183).

Spicy coconut sauce

Masaledar naryal salan

Preparation and cooking time: *Makes up to 1.1 L/2pt sauce*
   about 50 minutes

1 coconut
1 medium-sized red pepper, seeded, cored and chopped
6 garlic cloves, peeled and chopped
75 g/3 oz parsley, chopped
2 tablespoons freshly ground black pepper
1 teaspoon salt

Heat the oven to 200C/400F/gas 6.

Bake the coconut for 15 minutes.

Place the hot coconut on concrete or another hard surface and smash it open with a hammer.

When the coconut pieces are cool enough to handle, peel away the brown papery skin from the white meat with a potato peeler. Chop any large pieces, if necessary, into smaller ones.

Put the coconut meat and the rest of the ingredients and 150 ml/5 fl oz water in a food processor or blender, in batches, and with a little extra water if necessary, and liquify the mixture.

Thin the coconut mixture with 1 L/1¾pt water.

Spicy coconut prawns

Naryal jhinga masaledar

Preparation and cooking time: *Serves 4*
  making the masala*, *plus 15 minutes*

450g/1 lb shelled raw shrimp, cleaned, washed and dried
150 ml/5 fl oz mustard oil
4 bay leaves, crumbled
1 medium-sized onion, peeled and chopped
¼ teaspoon salt
12 cherry or 6 small tomatoes, quartered
For the masala
meat of 1 fresh coconut, broken into small pieces (page 52)
6 garlic cloves
4 cm/1½in ginger root, cut into 2–3 pieces
5–6 green chillies, seeded (optional)
1 tablespoon chopped fresh parsley
4 tablespoons vinegar
4 bay leaves

Combine the *masala* ingredients in a food processor for about 2 minutes and reserve.

Heat the oil in a small frying-pan over low heat. When hot, add the onion and bay leaves and cook, stirring occasionally, until the onion softens.

Add the *masala*, stir and cook for 2–3 minutes.

Add the shrimp and cook for 1 minute, stirring all the while.

Add the tomatoes and salt, cover and continue cooking for 3–4 minutes. Stir and serve with plain boiled rice.

* spice mixture

Mackerel sautéed with mustard and dill

Rai aur suwa ki bhuni machli

Preparation and cooking time: about 15 minutes   Serves 4–6

3 × 575g/1¼lb mackerels, cleaned, discarding head and tail
juice of 2 large lemons
5 tablespoons Dijon mustard
4 large garlic cloves, peeled and chopped
4 bay leaves, crumbled
8 tablespoons vegetable oil
½ teaspoon cayenne pepper
½ teaspoon salt
4–5 tablespoons chopped fresh dill

Cut the fish across into steaks, each about 4cm/1½in thick.

Combine the lemon juice, mustard, garlic, bay leaves, cayenne pepper and salt in a bowl, then add the mackerel steaks and stir to coat them.

Heat the oil in a frying-pan over low heat, add the mackerel mixture and sauté it gently for 10–12 minutes, turning once, or until the fish is done.

Sprinkle over the dill and serve with Green pea pillau (page 180).

Baked mackerel and tomatoes

Tamatar walli dum machli

Preparation and cooking time: 25 minutes   *Serves 4–6*

3 × 575g/1¼lb mackerel, cleaned, discarding head and tail
4 tablespoons vegetable oil
1 tablespoon caraway seeds
12 cherry or 6 small tomatoes
4 tablespoons vinegar
¼ teaspoon salt
1 teaspoon chilli powder

Cut the fish across into steaks, each about 4cm/1½in thick.

Heat half the oil in a large frying-pan over low heat, add the caraway seeds and cook for 3–4 minutes.

Add the mackerel steaks, then place the tomatoes on top of the fish.

Combine the vinegar, the rest of the oil, salt and chilli powder and pour the mixture over the fish and tomatoes. Cover and cook over low heat for 15 minutes or until done. Serve with Yellow turmeric rice (page 186).

Baked red snapper

Dum ki lal machli

Preparation and cooking time: about 1 hour   *Serves 3–4*

1.1 kg/2½lb red snapper, cleaned
vegetable oil for greasing
4 tablespoons lemon juice
1 tablespoon caraway seeds
1 hot green chilli, sliced and seeded (optional)
salt and freshly ground black pepper

Heat the oven to 180C/350F/gas 4.

Place the fish in a greased baking tin. Sprinkle over 2 table-spoons of the lemon juice, then sprinkle over ½ teaspoon of the caraway seeds, ½ of the sliced chilli and a pinch each of salt and pepper.

Turn the fish over and repeat with the rest of the ingredients, and bake for 45 minutes. Serve with Cashew rice (page 187).

* You can also substitute smaller whole firm-fleshed fish in this recipe, such as mackerel or mullet.

Grilled halibut

Machli ka tikka

This is my favourite way to cook halibut, and it also produces delicious results with other flat fish such as turbot and haddock.

Preparation and cooking time: about 25 minutes   *Serves 5–6*

4 tablespoons lemon juice
1.4 kg/3 lb halibut steak, about 4 cm/1½ thick, sliced into serving portions
1 tablespoon parsley flakes or 3 tablespoons chopped fresh parsley
½ teaspoon freshly ground black pepper
pinch of salt
3 garlic cloves, peeled and thinly sliced
vegetable oil for greasing
3–4 parsley sprigs, to garnish
3–4 lemon slices, to garnish

Heat the grill to high. Rub the lemon juice into the fish.

Coat the fish with parsley, pepper, salt and garlic, both sides. The garlic will adhere if sliced thinly enough.

Place the fish in a foil-lined, then greased baking tin. When ready, place the fish about 18 cm/7 in under the grill and cook for 8 minutes.

Turn the fish over and continue cooking for 8 minutes or until the fish is done but not dry and overcooked.

Garnish with parsley sprigs and lemon slices and serve with Chilli-tomato salad (page 173-4).

Pan-braised haddock

Tali hui machli

Preparation and cooking time: 15–20 minutes   *Serves 2–3*

4 tablespoons olive oil
3 teaspoons Dijon mustard
½ teaspoon cumin seeds
pinch of salt
2 bay leaves, crumbled
¼ teaspoon freshly ground black pepper
900g/2 lb haddock, salmon or other fish steaks
2 garlic cloves, peeled and thinly sliced

Combine the olive oil, mustard, cumin seeds, salt, bay leaves and black pepper.

Transfer the mixture to a large frying-pan over medium heat, then add the fish steaks in one layer.

Add the garlic slices and 150 ml/5 fl oz hot water. Cover the pan and cook over medium-low heat for 10–12 minutes, or until the fish flakes easily with a fork but remains moist. Serve with Green pea pillau (page 180) and a mixed salad.

Baked trout in mushroom vinaigrette

Kumbhi dam ki machli

Preparation and cooking time: 45 minutes   *Serves 3–4*

1 tablespoon Dijon mustard
2 tablespoons vinegar, lemon juice or dry sherry
1 tablespoon vegetable oil, plus extra for greasing and basting
3–4 trout, each about 350g/12oz, cleaned
125g/4oz large button mushrooms
½ teaspoon freshly ground black pepper
¼ teaspoon salt

Heat oven to 180C/350F/gas 4.

Place the fish and mushrooms in a greased baking tin. Whisk together the mustard, vinegar and oil and pour the mixture over the trout and mushrooms.

Sprinkle over the salt and pepper, and bake for 20 minutes, basting with a little extra oil, until the fish is done. Serve with plain boiled rice.

Baked stuffed carp
Shikampur machli

Preparation and cooking time: about 30 minutes   *Serves 4*

1.8 kg/4 lb carp, cleaned
6 spring onions, finely chopped
2 garlic cloves, finely chopped
vegetable oil for greasing
4 tablespoons lemon juice
¼ teaspoon salt
1 tablespoon dried parsley or 2 tablespoons chopped fresh parsley
½ teaspoon cayenne pepper
12 cherry or 6 small tomatoes

Heat the oven to 180C/350F/gas 4. Stuff the fish with the spring onions and garlic.

Place the fish in a foil-lined, greased baking tin and cover both sides of the fish with lemon juice, salt, parsley and cayenne pepper.

Place the fish in the oven for 10 minutes.

Place the tomatoes around the fish and bake another 10–15 minutes and serve with Cardamom and coriander rice (page 179).

* As an alternative, grey mullet can be substituted for carp in this recipe.

Fish pillau

Machli ka pullao

Preparation and cooking time: 30–35 minutes   *Serves 4–6*

2 tablespoons vegetable oil
1 medium-sized onion, peeled and chopped
8 cloves
2 garlic cloves, peeled and chopped
½ teaspoon salt
pinch of turmeric
400g/14oz long-grain rice
400–450g/14–16oz cod, salmon, turbot, plaice or similar fish flesh cut
    into bite-sized pieces
4 small tomatoes

Heat the oil in a large saucepan over medium-low heat. When hot, add the onion and cook, stirring occasionally, until it softens but does not brown. Add the cloves, garlic, salt, turmeric and 1.7L/3pt water. Bring to boil, add the rice and lower the heat to a simmer. Cover and cook until the water is almost all absorbed, about 15 minutes.

Add the fish and tomatoes, stir and cover for 5–8 minutes or until the rice and fish are cooked. Serve right away.

* Leftover cooked fish can be used in this dish, too, by adding the fish when the rice is ready and off the heat. Stir in the fish, cover and let it heat through for 2–3 minutes before serving.

Mustard prawns

Sarson-walla jhingha

Preparation and cooking time: 15 minutes   *Serves 4*

450g/1 lb shelled raw prawns, washed and dried
4 tablespoons vegetable oil
1½ tablespoons Dijon mustard
½ teaspoon caraway seeds
½ teaspoon chilli powder
4 tablespoons lemon juice
pinch of salt

Heat the oil in a small frying-pan over low heat. When hot, add the caraway seeds and chilli powder and cook for 3–4 minutes.

Add the prawns, mustard, salt and lemon juice and stir well. Cover the pan and cook for 5–6 minutes.

Stir the mixture well and serve with Saffron-pillau (page 183) and a green salad.

Baked sea bass with cumin and tomatoes

Zeera aur tamatar-walli rawas

Preparation and cooking time: 30–40 minutes　　　　　　*Serves 6*

125 ml/4 fl oz Dijon mustard
¼ teaspoon salt
4 garlic cloves, cleaned and chopped
1 tablespoon cumin seeds
1.8–2.7 kg/4–6 lb sea bass, cleaned
vegetable oil for greasing
12 cherry or 6 small tomatoes

Heat the oven to 170C/325F/gas 3. Combine the mustard, salt, garlic and cumin seeds.

Place the bass into a foil-lined, greased baking tin and pour the mustard sauce over it. Add the tomatoes to the tin, cover and bake for 20–30 minutes or until the fish is done but not over-cooked and dry. Serve with lemon wedges and Basmati pillau (page 185) or new potatoes.

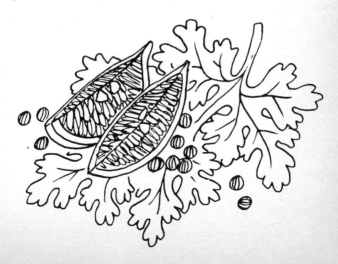

Yoghurt prawns
Dahi-walla jhingha

Preparation and cooking time: 15 minutes   *Serves 6*

75 ml/3 fl oz vegetable oil
4 garlic cloves, chopped
1 tablespoon ground cumin
1 tablespoon chilli powder
¼ teaspoon salt
24 shelled raw jumbo prawns, cleaned, washed and dried
225 ml/8 fl oz plain yoghurt

Heat the oil in a frying-pan over medium-low heat. When hot, add the garlic, cumin, chilli powder and salt and cook for 5 minutes or until the garlic begins to brown.

Add the dried prawns and cook for 2–3 minutes, stirring.

Add the yoghurt, stir, and continue cooking for 5 minutes. Serve with Raw spinach salad (page 176).

Prawns with mustard and dill

Rai-walla jhingha

Preparation and cooking time: *Serves 6–8*
  cleaning, then marinating the prawns, plus 10 minutes

900g/2lb raw prawns
200g/7oz Dijon mustard
2 teaspoons cayenne pepper
2 garlic cloves, finely chopped
1 teaspoon caraway seeds
¼ teaspoon turmeric
salt
4 tablespoons vegetable oil
1 large bunch of fresh dill, finely chopped

Shell and clean the prawns. Rinse them well, drain, pat them dry with kitchen paper and set aside.

Combine the mustard, cayenne pepper, garlic, caraway seeds, turmeric and salt to taste. Add the prawns and blend well. Cover and refrigerate for at least 1 hour and up to 6 hours.

Heat the oil in a deep frying-pan over medium-low heat. When hot, add the prawns, shaking them to remove most of the marinade, stir well, cover and cook for 3–4 minutes or until they just become firm.

Sprinkle over the dill and stir it in well, then serve the prawns right away with boiled rice and the remaining marinade as a sauce.

Spicy fish curry

Machli ka salan

Preparation and cooking time: 20–25 minutes   *Serves 4–6*

700g/1½lb cod or other white fish steaks, skin removed
about 6 tablespoons vegetable oil
2 large onions, peeled and halved, then sliced thinly
½ teaspoon ground coriander
¼ teaspoon turmeric
1 teaspoon chilli powder
½ teaspoon ground ginger
6 garlic cloves, pressed or very finely chopped
1 large tomato, chopped
½ teaspoon salt
125ml/4fl oz plain yoghurt
1 teaspoon sugar

Cut the fish into large bite-sized pieces. Heat 3 tablespoons of the oil in a frying-pan over medium heat. When hot, add the pieces of fish and lightly brown them quickly on all sides, adding a little more oil if necessary. Remove the pan from the heat, remove the fish from the pan and reserve.

Heat 3 tablespoons of oil in the same pan over medium-low heat and, when hot, cook the onions until they are light brown, stirring occasionally.

Add the coriander, turmeric, ginger and garlic and cook for 2–3 minutes.

Add the tomato and salt, and cook until the tomato is soft, adding 1 tablespoon water at a time if the spices stick. Stir in the yoghurt and sugar and simmer gently for 5 minutes.

Add the fish, stir in well to heat through and serve immediately with plain boiled rice.

* This curry is also good with mackerel, salmon, haddock or mullet.

Prawn pillau

Jhingha pullao

Preparation and cooking time: 50–60 minutes   *Serves 6*

425 g/15 oz basmati rice
25 mm/1 in fresh ginger root, grated
4 green chillies, seeded (optional) and finely chopped
1 teaspoon chilli powder
¼ teaspoon turmeric
¼ teaspoon ground coriander
8 garlic cloves, finely chopped
4 tablespoons lemon juice
150 ml/5 fl oz vegetable oil
2 medium-sized onions, peeled and chopped
2 cinnamon sticks, broken into pieces
12 cloves
24 large prawns, shelled, cleaned, washed and dried
4 tablespoons dried parsley or 40 g/1½ oz chopped fresh parsley

Put the rice in a bowl and wash it in several changes of cold water. Cover it with plenty of fresh water and let it soak for 30 minutes.

Meanwhile, combine the ginger, chillies, chilli powder, turmeric, coriander, garlic and lemon juice to make a paste and reserve.

Heat the oil in a large, heavy-based saucepan over medium-low heat. When hot, add the onions, cinnamon and cloves and sauté until the onion is beginning to brown, stirring occasionally.

Add the paste to the sautéed onion mixture with 175 ml/6 fl oz water and simmer for 8–10 minutes.

Add the prawns and continue cooking over low heat for 2 minutes.

Remove the prawns from pan with a slotted spoon and set them aside.

Add 575 ml/1 pt hot water to the spice mixture in the pan and bring it to the boil.

Drain the rice well, then add it to the pan, stirring well. Cover the pan very tightly and cook over low heat for 15 minutes or until the water is absorbed.

Remove the pan from the heat, stir the reserved prawns into the rice, cover and let the prawns finish cooking in the heat of the rice for 5–10 minutes.

Sprinkle with the parsley and serve.

Poultry and eggs

Chicken has always been one of my favourite dishes. When I was a little boy, my father took me to the bazaar where there were twenty or thirty chickens cooped up in large straw baskets. The chicken seller greeted my father and asked, 'Would you like three or four today?' and my father demanded to see one first. When the seller plucked out one chicken from the straw basket, all the other chickens clucked and squawked. There was quite a din in the bazaar because other chicken salesmen were picking birds out of their cages, too. The salesman held the chicken upside down by its legs and lifted its wing up. The salesman asked my father to feel how plump and meaty the breasts were. My father then bought three or four chickens, which were removed (screaming and carrying on) from the straw basket. We proceeded to the part of the bazaar where the chickens were slaughtered and left in a straw basket to drain. Then the chickens were plucked and cut into pieces. These chicken expeditions occurred twice a week, one of them usually at the weekend. I was always fascinated by the idea of picking out a chicken, examining it, seeing it slaughtered, brought home and prepared. (Sometimes the chickens would even have a marvellous bag of eggs inside.) When I was a child, we didn't have a refrigerator, so everything was prepared fresh from the market and cooked the same day, except for pickles and chutneys. These were made in large quantities and sealed in jars, so they would last a year or so.

If you have important guests for dinner in India, you serve chicken, almost as beef is served in the West for such occasions. Indians consider chicken a dish for the well-to-do. In India, when my college friends would come home with me for dinner, I would always request several chicken dishes, including chicken biriyani made with basmati rice, saffron, yoghurt, ginger, garlic, fresh mint and coriander. The combination of these ingredients created an extraordinary aroma, which we smelled while waiting for dinner.

When I go to buy chicken now, I still look for the same excitement I felt in the bazaar. Unfortunately I doubt that I can relive my childhood memories of chicken. I certainly don't relive them when I walk into a supermarket and see chickens which have been pre-packaged months earlier in plastic and frozen. Once I went to a farmer near my home in New York, and bought two fresh chickens. He slaughtered them in front of me and cleaned them, and with child-like excitement I brought them home and cooked them immediately. But it turned out that they were old roosters and so tough that they took a much longer time to cook than I could spare, and in the end I had to throw them both away.

Caraway-cayenne roast chicken

Shazeera-walla murgh mussallam

Preparation and cooking time: *Serves 4–6*
  making the stuffing (optional), plus about 1½ hours

1.4 kg/3 lb chicken
¾ lemon
½ teaspoon salt
½–1 teaspoon cayenne pepper
1 teaspoon caraway seeds
vegetable oil for greasing

Heat the oven 150C/300F/gas 2. Squeeze the lemon over the chicken and place the rind in the chicken cavity (or fill cavity with stuffing). Sprinkle with salt and pepper, then with caraway seeds.

Place the bird in a greased baking tin and roast it for 1½ hours or until done.

Serve with Lemon lentils (page 192-3) and Raw spinach salad (page 176).

Chilli-ginger roast chicken
Mirch-adrak-walla murgh mussallam

Preparation and cooking time: Serves 6
  making the stuffing, plus about 1 hour 20 minutes

5 cm/2 in fresh ginger root
2–4 garlic cloves, peeled
2 hot green chillies, seeded (optional)
4 tablespoons vinegar
¼ teaspoon salt
1.4 kg/3 lb chicken
stuffing of your choice (see recipes)
1 tablespoon vegetable oil plus extra for greasing

Heat the oven to 150C/300F/gas 2. Grate the ginger and garlic and finely chop the chillies, then mix them with the vinegar and salt — or combine these ingredients in a food processor.

Rub the chicken with half the oil. Stuff the chicken with one of the following stuffing mixtures, and place it in a greased baking tin. Rub the skin with the oil and spread the ginger and garlic mixture over the chicken.

Bake for 1½ hours or until the meat is done. Serve with Pistachio raita (page 170) and Kichri rice (page 181).

Lemon, ginger and chilli stuffing for chicken

Nimboo adrak aur mirch ka murgh mussallam

Preparation and cooking time: To fill a 900g–1.4kg/2–3lb chicken
5–10 minutes

2 green chillies, seeded (optional)
1 lemon, seeded and chopped
5cm/2in fresh ginger root, peeled and chopped
¼ teaspoon salt
½ teaspoon freshly ground black pepper
225g/8oz dry breadcrumbs
1 teaspoon caraway seeds

Combine the chillies, lemon, ginger, salt and pepper in food processor, or chop them together well.

Blend the breadcrumbs and caraway seeds into the chillies mixture thoroughly.

Chilli and parsley stuffing for chicken

Mirch aur kothmeer ka masala

Preparation time: 5 minutes   *To fill a 900g–1.4 kg/2–3 lb chicken*

125 ml/4 fl oz yoghurt
2 dried red chillies, seeded (optional) and finely chopped
¼ teaspoon chilli powder
¼ teaspoon salt
1 teaspoon parsley flakes or 3 tablespoons chopped fresh parsley
225 g/8 oz dry breadcrumbs

Mix together the yoghurt, chopped chillies, chilli powder, salt and parsley.

Blend the breadcrumbs into the mixture.

Pancakes and chutney stuffing for chicken

Chilla aur chutni-walla murgh

Preparation time: *To fill a 900g–1.4kg/2–3lb chicken*
   making the pancakes, plus 5 minutes

2 tablespoons Coconut and mint chutney (page 224)
25mm/1 in fresh ginger root, peeled and grated
1 green chilli, seeded (optional) and chopped
75 ml/3 fl oz vinegar
1 teaspoon salt
225 g/8 oz fresh, cold pancakes, torn into small pieces

Combine the chutney, grated ginger, chilli, vinegar and salt well,
then mix thoroughly into the pancakes.

Minced meat and giblet stuffing for chicken

Qeema masale-walla murgh

Preparation time: *To fill a 900g–1.4kg/2–3lb chicken*
    making the minced meat, plus 5 minutes

350ml/12floz mince with peas Kashmiri-style (page 124)
25mm/1in fresh ginger root, peeled and grated
3 tablespoons vegetable oil
1 teaspoon salt
the giblets from the chicken, chopped
1 green chilli, seeded (optional) and chopped
125g/4oz crustless good wholemeal bread, cut into small pieces

Combine the minced meat, ginger, vegetable oil, salt, chopped chilli and giblets. Add the bread and mix thoroughly.

Ginger chicken

Adrak-walli murgh

Preparation and cooking time: 45 minutes   *Serves 4*

4 tablespoons vegetable oil
1.4 kg/3 lb chicken, cut into small pieces
2 medium-sized onions, peeled and chopped
2 garlic cloves, peeled and chopped
2 cinnamon sticks
5 cm/2 in ginger root, peeled and grated
1 pinch saffron in 150 ml/5 fl oz hot water
2 teaspoons freshly ground black pepper
1 teaspoon salt
4–6 small tomatoes
4 tablespoons vinegar

Heat the oil in a large heavy-based frying-pan or saucepan over medium-high heat, and when hot, add the chicken pieces. Turn them frequently until they are lightly browned on all sides, then remove them with a slotted spoon, shaking off the oil, and reserve the pieces.

Stir the onions, garlic, cinnamon and ginger into the pan, lower the heat to medium and stir frequently until the onions begin to brown, 5–7 minutes.

Return the chicken to the pan with the saffron-water and season with salt and pepper. Add the tomatoes and vinegar to the pan, cover and cook over low heat for 20–25 minutes or until the meat is very tender. Serve with Yellow turmeric rice (page 186).

Tandoori chicken

Tandoori murgh

At first Christopher Reeve seemed reluctant to try 'spicy cooking', but eventually he happily freed himself from being victim of the propaganda against Indian food. His other favourites besides Tandoori chicken are Ginger chicken (page 77), Spiced okra (page 157-8) and Clove-garlic mixed vegetables (page 148).

Preparation and cooking time: *Serves 4*
  2 hours for overnight marinating, plus about 1 hour

5 cm/2 in fresh ginger root, peeled and grated
4 garlic cloves, peeled and grated
1 teaspoon cumin seed
½ teaspoon cayenne pepper
¼ teaspoon salt
225 ml/8 fl oz plain yoghurt
1.8 kg/4 lb chicken, cut into serving pieces
2 tablespoons vegetable oil
½ teaspoon turmeric

Combine grated ginger, garlic, cumin seed, cayenne pepper, salt and yoghurt.

Put the chicken pieces in a foil-lined baking tin, pour over the yoghurt mixture and use your hands to coat the meat completely. Leave the chicken to marinate for at least 2 hours or preferably overnight.

Heat the oven to 180C/350F/gas 4. Dribble the oil over the chicken in the baking tin, and sprinkle the chicken with turmeric. Place the pan in the oven and bake for about 1 hour, basting frequently with the oil and yoghurt marinade at the bottom of the pan. Serve with hot pitta bread and Lemon lentils (page 192-3).

Chicken breasts sautéed with chilli and cinnamon

Murgh kabab

Preparation and cooking time: 25 minutes   *Serves 4–6*

125 g/4 oz butter
1 large onion, peeled and chopped
1 cinnamon stick, broken up
8 boneless chicken breasts, cut in halves lengthways
125 ml/4 oz lemon juice
1 teaspoon salt
1 teaspoon freshly ground black pepper
1 green chilli, seeded (optional) and chopped
2 tablespoons dried parsley or 25 g/1 oz chopped fresh parsley

Melt the butter in a heavy-based frying-pan over medium-low heat. When hot, sauté the onions with the cinnamon until the onions begin to soften, 5–7 minutes, stirring occasionally.

Add the chicken breasts, lemon juice, salt and pepper and continue cooking for 8 minutes, stirring occasionally.

Add the chilli and parsley, lower the heat and cook for another 8–10 minutes, or until the meat is done.

Serve with Basmati pillau (page 185).

Yoghurt chicken 1
Dahi murgh 1

Preparation and cooking time: 1 hour 20 minutes   *Serves 10–12*
125 ml/4 oz vegetable oil
2 medium-sized onions, peeled and chopped
4 dried whole red chillies
12 cloves
2.7 kg/5½ lb chicken drumsticks and thighs
25 mm/1 in fresh ginger root, peeled and grated
350 ml/12 fl oz plain yoghurt
1 teaspoon salt
1 tablespoon freshly ground black pepper

Heat the oil in a large heavy-based frying-pan or saucepan over medium heat. When hot, add the onions, chillies and cloves, and cook, stirring frequently until the onions brown.

Add the chicken and ginger and stir continually until the meat is seared on all sides.

Mix the yoghurt and 225 ml/8 fl oz water together and add them to the pan with salt and pepper.

Cover and cook over medium-low heat, stirring occasionally, for 1 hour. Serve with Savoury onion rice (page 184) and Dressed green salad (page 174).

Yoghurt chicken 2
Dahi murgh 2

Preparation and cooking time:1 hour 20 minutes   *Serves 10–12*

125 ml/4 fl oz vegetable oil
2 medium-sized onions, peeled and chopped
1 bay leaf, crumbled
2.7 kg/5½ lb chicken drumsticks and thighs
2 teaspoons cumin seeds
350 ml/12 fl oz plain yoghurt
1½ teaspoons cayenne pepper
1 teaspoon salt
1 large tomato, quartered

Heat the oil in a large heavy-based frying-pan or saucepan over medium heat. When hot, add the onions and bay leaf, and cook, stirring frequently, until the onions brown.

Add the chicken and cumin seeds and stir continually until the meat is seared on all sides.

Blend the yoghurt and 125 ml/4 fl oz water together and add them to the pan with the cayenne pepper and salt.

Add the quartered tomato, cover and cook over a medium flame, stirring occasionally, for 1 hour. Serve with Basmati pillau (page 185) and Pistachio raita (page 170).

Chicken korma

Murgh korma

Preparation and cooking time: about 40 minutes   *Serves 4–6*

125 ml/4 fl oz cooking oil
2 medium-sized onions, peeled and chopped
4 whole dried red chillies
2 cinnamon sticks, broken up
6 cloves
1.1–1.4 kg/2½–3 lb chicken, skinned and cut up
275 ml/10 fl oz yoghurt
½ teaspoon salt
4 teaspoons freshly ground black pepper
450 g/1 lb fresh or frozen peas

Heat the oil in a large saucepan over medium-low heat. When hot, add the onions, chillies, cinnamon and cloves, and cook, stirring frequently, until the onions brown.

Add the chicken pieces and stir frequently until the meat is seared on all sides.

Mix the yoghurt with 275 ml/10 fl oz water and add this to the saucepan with the salt and pepper. Cover and cook over low heat for 20 minutes.

Add the peas, cover and cook for a further 10 minutes.

Serve right away with Basmati pilau (page 185) and Tomato mint raita (page 175).

Spicy mustard chicken

Masale-walli rai murgh

Felicity Kendal is always fond of this dish, which I prepare for her. She always asks for Lemon Lentils (page 192-3) and Cucumber raita (page 139) too.

Preparation and cooking time: 1 hour   *Serves 6–8*

125 ml/4 fl oz vegetable oil
2 medium-sized onions, peeled and chopped
7 cloves
2 × 1.1 kg/2½ lb chickens, cut through the bones into small pieces
1 teaspoon salt
1 teaspoon freshly ground black pepper
½ teaspoon chilli powder
2 tablespoons Dijon mustard
125 ml/4 fl oz tarragon vinegar

Heat the oil in a large heavy-based frying-pan or saucepan over medium heat. Add the onions and cloves, and cook, stirring frequently, until the onions brown.

Add the chickens, salt, pepper, chilli powder, mustard, vinegar and 425 ml/15 fl oz water.

Cook the mixture over low heat for 40–45 minutes, or until the meat is tender. Serve with plain boiled rice and Chicory-walnut salad (page 173).

Chicken in coconut sauce
Naryal-walla murgh

Shashi Kapoor has always been a great eater and enjoyed many, many of my meals in Cannes, London, New York, Claverack, Hyderabad and Bombay. Among his favourites in addition to Chicken in coconut are Basmati pillau (page 185) and Va-va-voom potatoes (page 137).

Preparation and cooking time: *Serves 6–8*
preparing the coconut, plus 1¼ hours

meat of ⅔ fresh coconut, in small pieces (see below)
2 green chillies, seeded (optional)
5 cm/2 in fresh ginger root, peeled
4 garlic cloves, peeled
2 tablespoons lemon juice
1½ teaspoons salt
2 × 1.1 kg/2½ lb chickens, cut through the bones into small pieces
125 ml/4 fl oz vegetable oil
2 medium-sized onions, cut into quarters
2 teaspoons freshly ground black pepper

Coarsely purée the coconut, chilli, ginger, garlic, lemon juice, salt and 125 ml/4 fl oz water in food processor or blender.

Place the chicken pieces in a large saucepan with the oil, onions, pepper, 225 ml/8 fl oz water and coconut purée.

Bring the liquid to a boil, then lower the heat and simmer gently for 1 hour, or until the meat is tender. Correct the seasoning and serve with plain boiled rice.

* To easily remove the meat from a fresh coconut, bake it first in a 200C/400F/gas 6 oven for 15 minutes. Place the hot coconut on concrete or other hard surface and smash it open with a hammer. When cool, peel away the brown papery skin with a potato peeler.

Tomato chicken

Tamatar murgh

Preparation and cooking time: about 1 hour   *Serves 6*

125 ml/4 fl oz vegetable oil
1 large onion, peeled and chopped
1 cinnamon stick, broken into pieces
4 black cardamom pods
1.4 kg/3 lb chicken, cut through the bones into about 10 small pieces
2 teaspoons caraway seeds
2 teaspoons freshly ground black pepper
½ teaspoon salt
4 large tomatoes, sliced
1 bunch fresh parsley, chopped

Heat the oil in a frying-pan over medium heat and when hot, add the onions, cinnamon and cardamom pods. Cook, stirring frequently, until the onions brown, about 5 minutes.

Add the chicken, caraway seeds, pepper and salt and stir over medium low heat for 15 minutes.

Add the tomatoes and chopped parsley, turn the heat to low and cook, stirring occasionally, for 30 minutes or until the chicken is tender. Serve with Basmati pillau (page 185).

Pepper chicken

Kali mirch murgh

Preparation and cooking time: 1–1¼ hours   *Serves 4*

125 ml/4 fl oz vegetable oil
2 medium-sized onions, chopped
7 black cardamom pods
1 teaspoon cumin seeds
1.4 kg/3 lb chicken, cut into pieces
juice of 2 medium-sized lemons
2 tablespoons freshly ground black pepper
2 tablespoons green peppercorn mustard
½ teaspoon salt
6 garlic cloves, peeled and pressed

Heat the oil in a heavy-based saucepan over medium heat. When hot, add the onions, cardamom pods and cumin seeds and cook, stirring frequently, until the onions begin to brown.

Add the chicken pieces, and cook, stirring frequently, for 10 minutes.

Combine the lemon juice, pepper, green peppercorn mustard and salt with 225 ml/8 fl oz water and pour the mixture over the chicken and onions. Let the mixture cook over medium-low heat for 15 minutes.

Add the garlic and continue cooking for 30–40 minutes, stirring occasionally, until the meat is tender, and adding a little more liquid if necessary to prevent burning. Serve with Basmati pillau (page 185) and Cucumber raita (page 139).

Richard's chicken

Richard ka khas murgh

Preparation and cooking time: 25 minutes   *Serves 4*

4 boneless chicken breasts
1 medium-sized onion, peeled and chopped
2 tablespoons oil
3–4 tablespoons Meaux or other coarse-grained mustard
1 cinnamon stick, broken in pieces
25 mm/1 in fresh ginger root, grated
1 tablespoon dried parsley or 3 tablespoons chopped fresh parsley
½ teaspoon cumin seeds
½ teaspoon turmeric
½ teaspoon salt
½ teaspoon coarsely ground pepper

Heat the oil in a frying- pan over medium heat. When hot, add the onions, cinnamon and ginger, and cook, stirring frequently, until the onions brown.

Cut the breasts into 2 lengthways, if they are large. Spread mustard over them very generously. Salt and pepper them and add them to the frying-pan with the onions.

Turn the heat to low and sprinkle cumin seeds, turmeric and parsley over them. Cook for 7–8 minutes.

Turn the meat over, cover the pan and cook a further 5 minutes or until the meat is done. Serve with Saffron pillau (page 183).

* A simple yet delicious sauce for chicken breasts can be made by gently heating 125 ml/4 fl oz each of coarse-grained mustard with whipping or heavy cream and pouring it over the sautéed meat.

Spicy chicken curry

Murgh masala

While we were shooting *Quartet* in Paris, Maggie Smith succumbed to my Spicy chicken curry, served with Cashew rice (page 187) and Spicy stewed cauliflower and potatoes (page 151). Later I prepared my Mackerel in coconut sauce (page 50) for her during the shooting of *A Room With A View*.

Preparation and cooking time: 30 minutes   *Serves 4*

3 tablespoons vegetable oil
1 large onion, sliced
6 peppercorns
1 cinnamon stick
4 cardamom pods
6 cloves
2 bay leaves, crumbled
1.4 kg/3 lb chicken, cut into pieces
¼ teaspoon turmeric
½ teaspoon chilli powder
½ teaspoon ground coriander
½ teaspoon ground cumin
½ teaspoon ground ginger
salt
2 garlic cloves, peeled and pressed
125 ml/4 fl oz plain yoghurt
½ teaspoon ground allspice

Heat the oil in a large saucepan over medium heat. When hot, add the onion, peppercorns, cinnamon, cardamom pods, cloves and bay leaves, and cook, stirring frequently, until the onions become light brown.

Add the chicken pieces and cook, stirring frequently, until the meat is seared on all sides.

Sprinkle in the turmeric, chilli powder, coriander, cumin, ginger and salt to taste, and stir in the garlic. Continue cooking, stirring occasionally, until the chicken is well coloured.

Add 425 ml/15 fl oz hot water, cover and simmer until the chicken is just cooked.

Add the yoghurt and allspice and simmer for 10 minutes. Serve with Green pea pillau (page 180) and Cucumber raita (page 139).

Chicken livers baked in spicy yoghurt

Dahi-walli murgh kalejee

Preparation and cooking time: 50 minutes   *Serves 4*

225 ml/8 fl oz plain yoghurt
1 teaspoon freshly ground black pepper
1 green chilli, seeded (optional) and finely chopped
4 garlic cloves, peeled and chopped
¼ teaspoon salt
2 tablespoons softened butter
450 g/1 lb chicken livers

Combine all the ingredients except the chicken livers in a small ovenproof dish.

Add the chicken livers in and marinate them for 15 minutes.

Heat the oven to 170C/325F/gas 3. Place the dish in the oven and bake for 30 minutes or until the livers are done, basting frequently with the yoghurt sauce. Serve with Raw spinach salad (page 176) and Yellow turmeric rice (page 186).

Chicken livers baked in spicy mustard

Rai-walli murgh kalejee

Preparation and cooking time: 50 minutes　　　　　　　*Serves 3–4*

450 g/1 lb chicken livers
225 ml/4 fl oz plain or flavoured Dijon mustard
1 teaspoon freshly ground black pepper
4 garlic cloves, peeled and chopped
2 tablespoons parsley flakes or 25 g/1 oz chopped fresh parsley
1 teaspoon cumin seeds
2 tablespoons softened butter

Combine all the ingredients except the chicken livers in a small ovenproof dish.

Add the chicken livers and leave them to marinate for 15 minutes.

Heat the oven to 170C/325F/gas 3. Place the dish in the oven and bake for 30 minutes or until the livers are done, basting frequently with the mustard sauce. Serve with Cashew rice (page 187).

Roast stuffed duck

Bathak mussallam

Preparation and cooking time: *Serves 4–5*
 making the stuffing, plus about 2 hours

2.3 kg/5 lb oven-ready duck with giblets
salt and freshly ground black pepper
stuffing (see recipe)
2 garlic cloves, peeled and pressed

Wash the giblets and set them to simmer in water to cover for 20–30 minutes to make a rich stock.

Meanwhile, wash duck thoroughly, then dry it. Remove any visible fat from the neck and rear vent.

Sprinkle salt inside the cavity, then fill it with stuffing and truss the duck (see below).

Rub in the pressed garlic and sprinkle 1 teaspoon or more pepper. Prick the breasts with a fork to allow the fat to escape during cooking.

Place the bird on a trivet or rack in a roasting pan and roast for 2 hours or until the duck juices run colourless. Baste often with the drippings and some of the giblet stock.

Serve the duck and stuffing with the rest of the warmed stock served separately. Serve with Watercress, celeriac and chicory salad (page 165) and roast potatoes.

* To truss the duck, pass a skewer through one wing of the duck, then through the neck flap and the other wing. Tie the legs together.

Ismail's duck stuffing

Khas bathak masala

Preparation time: 5 minutes   *To fill a 2.3 kg/5 lb duck*

3 tablespoons mustard
2 tablespoons vinegar
225 g/8 oz dried breadcrumbs
1 hot chilli, seeded (optional) and finely chopped
6 garlic cloves, peeled and chopped
1 apple, peeled, cored and sliced
½ teaspoon salt

Combine the mustard and vinegar, and stir in the breadcrumbs.
Add the chilli, garlic, apple and salt.

Roast stuffed goose

Qaaz mussallam

For Christmas, 1983, we had a big crowd, so I prepared two
5.4 kg/12 lb geese. They aren't as difficult to cook as one might
think — and they are delicious. They may make turkey seem
rather bland by comparison.

Prepare the goose for roasting as you would a turkey, except
you really must place it on a rack or trivet as it produces lots of
fat while cooking. Prick the goose to release the fat during
roasting.

5.4 kg/12 lb oven-ready goose
salt
stuffing (see recipe)
about 2 tablespoons freshly ground black pepper

Heat the oven to 170C/325F/gas 3. Wash the goose thoroughly, dry it and weigh it. Salt the inside and fill it with stuffing and place it on a rack or trivet in a large roasting tin.

Prick the goose about the breast and legs. Sprinkle *lots* of ground black pepper over the goose.

Roast for 20–25 minutes per pound, checking from time to time to spoon off the excess melted fat. (Cool, then refrigerate this superbly flavoured fat to use in cooking other dishes).

Serve the goose and stuffing with roast potatoes and Dressed green salad (page 174).

Spicy fruit goose stuffing

Phal-walli qaaj mussallam

Preparation time: 10 minutes   *To fill a 5.4 kg/12 lb goose*
225 g/8 oz dried breadcrumbs
6 small whole crab-apples
3 pears, peeled, cored and coarsely chopped
150 g/5 oz raisins or sultanas
1 teaspoon parsley flakes or 1 tablespoon chopped fresh parsley
125 ml/4 fl oz mustard
salt
1 tablespoon cayenne pepper
225 g/8 oz cooked potatoes, mashed
125 g/4 oz leftover Mince with peas Kashmiri-style (page 124), or
  chicken or goose giblets, chopped

Combine all ingredients in a large bowl.

Roast stuffed turkey

Feelmurgh mussallam

In the United States my friends always want turkey for Thanksgiving. It's always good, but turkey can sometimes be rather bland, so I make a spicy dressing to increase the pleasure of roast turkey.

Preparation and cooking time: *Serves 12–16*
  making the stuffing, plus 4¼–5¼ hours

5.4–6.8 kg/12–15 lb oven-ready turkey with giblets
salt
freshly ground black pepper

Wash the giblets and set them to simmer in water to cover for 20–30 minutes to make a rich stock.

Heat the oven to 150C/300F/gas 2. Wash the bird thoroughly, then dry it.

Rub inside with salt and fill with stuffings (see recipes). Some cooks insist on sewing up the opening, but I am always in such a rush I don't have time.

Sprinkle with lots of black pepper, at least 1 tablespoon. To prevent the turkey from drying up, cover it with a cloth moistened in the giblet stock to hold in the moisture.

Roast the turkey for 20 minutes per pound, basting frequently with the giblet stock.

Spicy turkey stuffing

Tez feelmurgh ka masala

As you use the giblets for this stuffing, baste the roasting turkey
with olive or other vegetable oil.

Preparation and cooking time: *To fill a 5.4–6.8 kg/12–15 lb turkey*
   10–15 minutes

the turkey giblets, chopped
2 hot green chillies, seeded (optional)
2 medium-sized onions, peeled and chopped
4 tablespoons tarragon vinegar
4 tablespoons olive oil
6 garlic cloves, peeled
1 tablespoon parsley flakes or 3 tablespoons chopped fresh parsley
4 dry red chillies, seeded (optional)
350 g/12 oz dried breadcrumbs
25 g/1 oz walnuts
25 g/1 oz raisins

Combine giblets, green chillies, onions, tarragon vinegar, olive
oil, garlic, parsley flakes and red chillies in food processor.

Coarsely purée the giblets, the fresh green and dried red chillies,
onions, vinegar, oil, garlic and parsley in a food processor, or
chop them together well.

Blend the breadcrumbs thoroughly into the giblets mixture,
then mix in the walnuts and raisins.

Ismail's superb turkey stuffing
Khas feelmurgh ka masala

The first two ingredients I added to the breadcrumbs I found in the refrigerator. I encourage you to also be *adventurous* in creating your stuffings.

Preparation and cooking time: *To fill a 5.4–6.8 kg/12–15 lb turkey peeling the chestnuts, plus 10 minutes*

225 g/8 oz leftover cold Oxtail dal (page 196)
175 g/6 oz leftover Potatoes and peas (page 136)
125 g/4 oz dried breadcrumbs
1 large onion, peeled and chopped
2 green chillies, seeded (optional) and chopped
2 teaspoons cumin seeds
2 apples, peeled, cored and chopped
24 chestnuts, peeled and chopped
125 ml/4 fl oz vegetable oil
½ teaspoon salt
1 teaspoon freshly ground black pepper

Combine all the ingredients, mixing thoroughly.

Tomato-caraway egg curry

Tamatar shazeera-walla rasedar unde

Jennifer Kendal was a vegetarian and though she never cooked she was nevertheless very discerning about Indian cuisine. She loved Tomato-caraway egg curry and also Lemon lentils (page 192-3) and Broccoli in garlic-lemon butter (page 155). I enjoyed cooking for her.

Preparation and cooking time: 20 minutes　　　　　　　*Serves 4*

2 tablespoons vegetable oil
1 medium-sized onion, peeled and chopped
4 bay leaves, crumbled
3 large tomatoes, chopped
4 tablespoons vinegar
1/2 teaspoon salt
1/2 teaspoon cayenne pepper
1/2 teaspoon caraway seeds
8 eggs, hard-boiled, shelled and halved
4 tablespoons chopped fresh chives

Heat the oil in a saucepan over medium-low heat. When hot, add the onion and bay leaves and cook until the onion is tender, stirring occasionally.

Add tomatoes, vinegar, salt, cayenne pepper and caraway seeds, and simmer gently until the tomatoes are soft, about 10 minutes.

Add the halved eggs, cook 2–3 minutes to heat them through.

Sprinkle with the chives and serve with plain boiled rice, or warm pitta bread.

Clove curried eggs

Long-wale rasedar unde

Preparation and cooking time: Serves 4
  hard boiling the eggs, plus 25 minutes

75 ml/3 fl oz vegetable oil
2 medium-sized onions, peeled and chopped
16 black peppercorns
8 cloves
3 bay leaves, crumbled
1 large potato, peeled (optional) and cut into medium-sized dice
¼ teaspoon salt
2 tablespoons lemon juice or vinegar
2 teaspoons Dijon mustard, preferably lemon-flavoured
8 hard-boiled eggs, shelled
1 teaspoon parsley flakes or 1 tablespoon chopped fresh parsley

Heat the oil in a saucepan over medium-low heat. When hot, add the onion, peppercorns, cloves and bay leaves, and cook, stirring occasionally, until the onion is tender.

Add the diced potato and salt to the pan with 150 ml/5 fl oz hot water. Whisk together the lemon juice or vinegar and mustard and stir them into the saucepan. Simmer the mixture gently for 15 minutes or until the potato is tender, adding a little more water if necessary.

Halve the eggs and add them to the pan with the parsley. Cook for 2–3 minutes and serve with Saffron pillau (page 183).

Ismail's egg salad

Ismail ka unde cachumber

Preparation time: Serves 4–6
  hard boiling the eggs, plus 10 minutes

10 medium-sized, hard-boiled eggs, shelled and chopped
1 green chilli, seeded (optional) and chopped
4 spring onions, chopped
3 tablespoons mayonnaise
1 tablespoon Dijon mustard
salt and freshly ground black pepper to taste
lettuce leaves, to serve

Mix the ingredients together well and serve on lettuce leaves.

'Tortilla' eggs with parsley and chilli

Kothmiri unde roti

Preparation and cooking time: 10 minutes   Serves 2

4 medium-sized eggs
1 teaspoon dried parsley or 1 tablespoon chopped fresh parsley
1 small green chilli, seeded (optional) and chopped
salt and freshly ground black pepper
25g/1oz butter

Whisk the eggs with the parsley, chilli, and salt and pepper to taste.

Melt the butter in a small frying pan over low heat. When hot, pour in the egg mixture. Cook the mixture, rather like a Spanish tortilla, for 5 minutes or until it is as firm as you like. Serve with a green salad dressed with olive oil and lemon juice.

Omelette fines herbes

Sookhi patyoon ka aam-late

Preparation and cooking time: 10 minutes   *Serves 2–3*

6 medium-sized eggs
3 tablespoons butter
1 tablespoon fresh or 1 teaspoon dried fines herbes

Whisk the eggs together.

Melt the butter in a frying pan over low heat and add the whisked eggs.

When the eggs are *slightly* firm, sprinkle the herbs over them. After 3 minutes, use a spatula to turn half the omelette over on to the other half. Cook for 2 more minutes and serve. Serve with crusty bread.

Souffléd scrambled eggs

Khagina

Preparation and cooking time: 15 minutes   *Serves 2–3*

25 g/1 oz butter
1 medium-sized onion, peeled and chopped
2 garlic cloves, peeled and chopped
¼ teaspoon cayenne pepper
1 green chilli, seeded (optional) and chopped
2 small tomatoes, chopped
6 medium-sized eggs
1 tablespoon chopped fresh parsley

Heat the butter in a small frying-pan over medium-low heat. When melted, add the onion, and cook, stirring occasionally, until it begins to colour.

Add the garlic, cayenne pepper, chilli and tomatoes, stirring.

Quickly whisk the eggs as if to scramble, and add them to the pan. Sprinkle over the parsley, cover, turn the heat to low and cook for 10 minutes or until the mixture rises in the manner of a soufflé. Serve with crusty bread.

Scrambled mustard eggs

Rai ke unde

Preparation and cooking time: 10–12 minutes   *Serves 4*

25 g/1 oz butter
1 tablespoon Meaux or similar coarse-grained mustard
8 medium-sized eggs
1 tablespoon cream
pinch of cayenne pepper
pinch of salt

Melt the butter in a small frying pan over low heat. Add the mustard and cook for 3–4 minutes.

Whisk together the eggs with the cream, salt and pepper. Pour the mixture into the pan and stir. Cover and continue cooking for about 6 minutes, stirring occasionally. Don't let the eggs get too firm — they should be served soft. Serve with toast.

Ismail's eggs
Khas unde

Preparation and cooking time: *Serves 3–4*
  hard boiling the eggs, plus 8–10 minutes

6 medium-sized, hard-boiled eggs
2 tablespoons Dijon mustard
2 tablespoons wine vinegar
2 tablespoons olive oil
1 green chilli, seeded (optional) and chopped
2 tablespoons chopped fresh parsley
salt

Combine eggs, mustard, vinegar, olive oil, chilli and parsley.

Cook over low flame for about 3 minutes. Turn, and cook a further 2 minutes. Serve immediately with crusty French bread.

* The above spice ingredients may be processed with a steel knife in a food processor if desired, for about 4 seconds.

Meat

As Muslims, we are great meat-eaters, so meat was a part of our everyday cooking at home. It was served at our main meal, usually with some kind of *roti* (bread) and rice. We generally ate goat, the most common meat in India, except in Kashmir where lamb is more frequently cooked. There are no roasts in Indian cookery. Kebabs, on the other hand, are cooked frequently and eaten with great enjoyment and there are many, many recipes for them. Basically, a kebab is mince combined with various flavourful ingredients and prepared in many ways. They can be meat patties cooked in a frying-pan, or wrapped around a skewer and grilled over a charcoal fire in the same way as cubes of lamb, which are really another kind of kebab. There are also liver kebabs, kidney kebabs and ox tongue kebabs.

I have given recipes in this book for lamb roasts, rib roasts and beef roasts, but the meat recipes I have created are usually not examples of traditional Indian cooking. In India, beef is eaten in restaurants and is prepared mainly in Muslim, Christian and Parsi households and in the luxury hotels catering to foreigners. Beef in India comes mainly from water buffalo and bulls. Hindus, the majority of Indians, consider cows sacred and you will rarely see a Hindu eating a dish prepared from beef, except Westernized Hindus living in India or, more likely, outside the country.

In our household, beef was a great treat at home on Id-Uz-Zuha, a Muslim festival somewhat like the American Thanksgiving. Every Muslim family traditionally has to make a sacrifice on that day, of a cow, a camel, a goat or a lamb. Naturally, more spiritual benefits are derived for the family from the slaughter of a large animal like a steer than from a mere goat. Fortunately nothing goes to waste in India; every part of the sacrificial animal is used in some way or another, rather in the same way as the thrifty French would do.

It is not essential to eat meat every day, though I have some friends who say they need it every day to give them energy and sustaining power for their creative work. Regardless of how often my friends enjoy meat, all of them agree with me that it should never be overcooked. Meat should be tender and juicy, not cooked until it is falling apart or on the point of drying out. This is important, for over the years whenever a well-prepared, well-cooked roast was brought to the table, I have enjoyed seeing the delight and satisfaction on the faces of my friends — and that of course is one the very best reasons to cook.

Baked lamb with chilli and ginger
Dabba gosht

Preparation and cooking time: about 1 hour　　　　*Serves 6–8*

10–15 green chillies, seeded
5 tablespoons vegetable oil, plus extra for greasing
6 pieces 25 mm/1 in fresh ginger root, peeled, chopped and crushed in a
　　garlic press
900 g/2 lb boneless lean lamb, cut in bite-sized dice
salt
4 large tomatoes, coarsely chopped
1 large potato, boiled
3 tablespoons chopped coriander leaves
4 medium-sized eggs
For the ground spice mixture
2 cardamom pods
2 cinnamon sticks, broken in pieces
6 cloves
½ teaspoon cumin seeds
8–10 black peppercorns

Purée the seeded chillies into a paste with 2 tablespoons of the vegetable oil in a food processor or blender and set aside.

Extract the juice from the pieces of ginger root by putting them through a garlic press. Reserve the juice and discard the pulp.

Put the lamb in a saucepan, cover with water and bring to a boil. Immediately drain the meat in a sieve and discard the water. Rinse the lamb and return it to the pan with the chilli purée and ginger juice.

Season the mixture with salt to taste, and add water just to cover. Bring the mixture to a boil, lower the heat and simmer until the lamb is tender, about 30 minutes, topping up with hot water as necessary.

Meanwhile, to make the spice mixture, grind the spices to a coarse powder in a pestle and mortar, food processor or coffee mill.

Heat the oven to 180C/375F/gas 5. When the meat is tender, raise the heat, rapidly boil off almost all the water and remove the pan from the heat. Stir in the tomatoes, boiled potato, peeled and diced, coriander leaves and ground spice mixture.

Grease a small roasting tin and spread the lamb mixture inside. Beat the eggs well and pour them evenly over the mixture. Heat the rest of the vegetable oil until it is smoking hot, and immediately pour it over the lamb mixture. Bake for 15 minutes or until the eggs are set, then serve hot with warmed pitta bread and Cucumber raita (page 139).

Cubed lamb with mustard and bay

Rai-walla boti gosht

Preparation and cooking time: about 1 hour   *Serves 4–6*

125 ml/4 fl oz vegetable oil
1 large onion, peeled and chopped
900 g/2 lb boneless lean lamb, cubed
6 bay leaves, crumbled
For the sauce
125 ml/4 fl oz English or other made hot mustard
2 teaspoons cayenne pepper
½ teaspoon salt
125 ml/4 fl oz lemon juice
250 ml/8 fl oz vinegar

Mix together the sauce ingredients and set them aside.

Heat half the oil in a large heavy saucepan over medium-high heat. When hot, brown the chopped onion quickly, stirring, and remove them with a slotted spoon and reserve.

Add the rest of the oil to the pan, and when hot, add the cubed meat, stirring it continually to brown it quickly on all sides.

Return the onion to the pan with the bay leaves, lower the heat to medium and cook for 10 minutes, stirring occasionally.

Add the sauce to the meat mixture, cover, turn the heat to low and cook for 35 minutes or until the meat is very tender. Serve with plain boiled rice.

Pan-roasted lamb

Bhuna gosht

Preparation and cooking time: *Serves 12*
    1 hour for marinating, plus 1¼ hours

2kg/4½lb boneless lean leg of lamb (about 3.2kg/7lb as a whole joint)
2 tablespoons fresh ginger root, finely chopped
3 hot green chillies, chopped with seeds
1 tablespoon peeled and finely chopped garlic
1½ tablespoons chopped coriander leaves
juice of 1 lemon
salt to taste
1 teaspoon freshly ground black pepper
1 tablespoon vegetable oil

Cut the meat into 4cm/1½in cubes.

Place the lamb in a bowl, add the remaining ingredients and mix them together. Set aside to marinate until you are ready to cook, but at least one hour.

Heat the oven to 180C/350F/gas 4.

Put the lamb mixture into a shallow roasting pan about 40 × 23cm/16 × 9in. Place the pan in the oven, uncovered, and bake 1¼ hours without stirring. The lamb should be tender with plenty of pan juices.

Serve the mixture with Basmati pillau (page 185) and a curly endive salad.

Rajasthani spicy lamb stew
Rajasthani gosht

Preparation and cooking time: 1¾ hours   *Serves 4*

4 tablespoons vegetable oil
450g/16oz boneless lean lamb, cut into 5cm/2in cubes
2 medium-sized onions, peeled and sliced
25mm/1in fresh ginger root, chopped
8 garlic cloves, peeled and chopped
1 teaspoon ground coriander
½ teaspoon ground cumin
½ teaspoon turmeric
125ml/4floz plain yoghurt, stirred
2 teaspoons chilli powder
salt

Heat half the oil in a saucepan over medium-high heat. When hot, add the cubed lamb and stir constantly to brown on all sides. Remove the meat with a slotted spoon and reserve it.

Add the rest of the oil to the pan, and when hot, add the onions and brown them, stirring frequently to prevent burning.

Meanwhile, mix the ginger, garlic, coriander, cumin and turmeric into the yoghurt. When the onions are browned, add the meat and yoghurt mixture to the pan, stirring. Reduce the heat to medium-low and simmer the mixture for 10 minutes, adding a little water if necessary to prevent burning.

Add the chilli powder to the pan, season with salt and add 425ml/15floz hot water to meat. Cover, lower the heat and simmer for 1¼ hours or until the meat is tender and the spicy gravy is thick. Serve with plain boiled rice.

Tomato lamb curry

Tamatar gosht

Preparation and cooking time: about 1½ hours   *Serves 3–4*

4 tablespoons vegetable oil
3 bay leaves, crumbled
25 mm/1 in piece of cinnamon stick
4 cloves
4 cardamom pods
4 peppercorns
450 g/1 lb boneless lean lamb, cut into large bite-sized pieces
1 large onion, peeled and grated
½ teaspoon ground ginger
½ teaspoon peeled and pressed or finely chopped garlic
¼ teaspoon turmeric
½ teaspoon ground coriander
1 teaspoon chilli powder
½ teaspoon salt
1 large tomato, finely chopped
1 tablespoon chopped coriander leaves

Heat the oil in a saucepan over medium heat. When hot, add the bay leaves, cinnamon, cloves, cardamom pods and peppercorns and cook until they begin to pop, 2–3 minutes.

Add the lamb and onion and cook, stirring, until the onions and the lamb are lightly browned.

Stir the ginger, garlic, turmeric, ground coriander, chilli powder and salt into the saucepan, turn the heat to medium-low and cook for 3–4 minutes.

Add the chopped tomato to the mixture, stirring well, and cook for 5 minutes or until the tomato becomes very soft.

Add 425 ml/15 fl oz hot water to the pan, bring to the boil, cover and simmer over low heat for 1 hour or until the meat is tender. Stir in the chopped coriander leaves and serve with Basmati pillau (page 185).

Spicy lamb stew

Rogan josh

Preparation and cooking time: about 1¼ hours   *Serves 4–6*

125 g/4 oz butter
2 medium-sized onions, peeled and chopped
1 cinnamon stick, broken up
6 cardamom pods
3 whole green chillies
6 garlic cloves, peeled and chopped
12 cloves
900 g/2 lb boneless lean lamb, cut into large bite-sized pieces
125 ml/4 fl oz plain yoghurt
1 tablespoon coarsely ground black pepper

Heat the butter in a saucepan over medium-low heat and when melted, add the onions and cook until the onions are soft, about 5 minutes, stirring occasionally.

Add the cinnamon, cardamom pods, chillies, garlic and cloves and continue cooking for 8–10 minutes, stirring occasionally.

Add the meat and continue cooking for 4–5 minutes, stirring occasionally.

Stir together the yoghurt, 125 ml/4 fl oz water and pepper, then stir the mixture into the saucepan. Cover the meat and cook gently for 45 minutes or until the meat is tender. Serve hot with Green pea pillau (page 180).

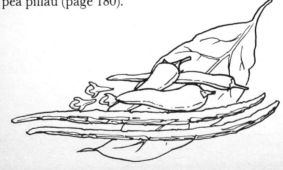

Roast lamb with ginger and caraway

Adrak aur shazeera-walli ran

Raquel Welch enjoyed this particular dish, which I prepared for her just before we began shooting *The Wild Party*.

Preparation and cooking time: *Serves 6–8*
  1–2 hours marinating, plus about 2 hours

3.2 kg/7 lb leg of lamb
salt
2 teaspoons dried parsley or 2 tablespoons chopped fresh parsley
For the marinade
125 ml/4 fl oz lemon juice
2 green chillies, seeded (optional)
6 dried red chillies, seeded (optional) and chopped
5 cm/2 in fresh ginger root, peeled and chopped
1 teaspoon chopped fresh parsley
1 tablespoon caraway seeds
3 large garlic cloves, peeled

Purée the marinade ingredients in a food processor or in a blender — if the latter, it may have to be done in batches.

Add salt to taste, then rub the marinade well over the lamb on all sides. Leave the meat to season for 1–2 hours.

Heat the oven to 230C/450F/gas 8.

Place the lamb and any marinade into a greased baking tin, sprinkle the meat with the parsley and cook in the oven for 30 minutes.

Reduce the heat to 200C/400F/gas 6 and cook for 1 hour or until done. Serve with warmed pitta bread and Cucumber raita (page 139).

Lamb with onions and tomatoes

Gosht do piyaza

Preparation and cooking time: 45 minutes   *Serves 4–6*

275–350 ml/10–12 fl oz vegetable oil
900 g/2 lb onions, peeled and sliced
6 black cardamom pods
900 g/2 lb boneless lean lamb, cut into large bite-sized pieces
6–8 small dried red chillies
225 ml/8 fl oz plain yoghurt
12 small whole tomatoes
½ teaspoon salt
1 tablespoon freshly ground black pepper

Heat the oil in a large heavy-based saucepan over medium heat. When hot, add the onions and cardamom pods, and cook, stirring, until they are slightly browned. Remove them from the pan with a slotted spoon and drain them on absorbent paper.

Add the lamb and chillies to the hot oil in the pan and stir continually until meat browns on all sides, about 5 minutes.

Return the onions to the pan, turn the heat to low and continue cooking for 10–15 minutes, stirring occasionally.

Add the yoghurt, tomatoes, salt and pepper, and cook over medium-low heat for another 15 minutes or until the lamb is tender. Serve with warmed pitta bread and Tomato mint raita (page 175), telling people to avoid the cardamom pods and chillies if wished.

North Indian lamb chops
Dahi-walli chap

Preparation and cooking time: 40 minutes　　　　　*Serves 4*

425 ml/15 fl oz plain yoghurt
½ teaspoon ground turmeric
1 teaspoon ground coriander
½ teaspoon salt
4 garlic cloves, peeled and finely chopped
125 ml/4 fl oz vegetable oil
4 small dried red chillies
1 cinnamon stick, broken up
1 tablespoon black mustard seeds
8 lamb chops
4 tablespoons chopped fresh coriander

Mix the yoghurt, turmeric, ground coriander, salt and garlic together in a bowl and reserve.

Heat the oil in a large saucepan over medium-low heat, and when hot, add the chillies, pieces of cinnamon stick and mustard seeds. Let them cook for 4–5 minutes.

Add the lamb chops and cook them for 8–10 minutes, turning them halfway through.

Pour in the yoghurt sauce and continue cooking over low heat for 15–18 minutes or until the meat is just tender. Sprinkle the chopped fresh coriander or parsley on top and serve with Saffron pillau (page 183) and a simple raita made of beaten plain yoghurt.

Crown roast of lamb, Merchant-style

Phasli ka taj

Preparation and cooking time: *Serves 10*
    45 minutes, plus roasting time

*3 best end of lamb joints, each with 6–8 cutlets, making a total of 20
    ribs (2 per person)*
vegetable oil for greasing
juice of 1 lemon
1 teaspoon dried or 1 tablespoon chopped fresh parsley
1 teaspoon salt
1 teaspoon black pepper
25 mm/1 in fresh ginger root, grated
For the stuffing
375 g/13 oz minced lamb (see below)
125 g/4 oz fresh white breadcrumbs
juice of 2 lemons
4–5 spring onions, finely chopped
*225 g/8 oz shelled fresh chestnuts, chopped, or canned unsweetened
    chestnuts, drained and chopped, or shelled walnuts*
salt and freshly ground black pepper

Have the butcher cut away the skin from the joints, then trim the
meat from the tops of the bones and have this minced to use for
some of the stuffing. Weigh the joints to calculate cooking time.

Then have the end bone of each joint sewed around, so that the
joints are attached. Bend the joints round, stitching the ends
together around the bones to form a crown. Tie up the crown
with kitchen string to hold the shape. Place the crown in a
greased roasting tin.

Heat the oven to 150C/300F/gas 2. Mix together some of the
minced lamb with the rest of the stuffing ingredients to just fill
the crown.

Combine the remaining ingredients and rub this evenly over the
meat.

Roast for 30 minutes per pound and serve with a mixed curly endive salad.

Beef rib roast, Merchant-style
Bhuna phasli

Preparation and cooking time: *Serves 4*
    marinating the meat, plus 2¼ hours

1.8 kg/4 lb fore rib joint
freshly ground black pepper
vegetable oil for greasing
For the marinade
5 cm/2 in piece of fresh ginger root, peeled and chopped
125 ml/4 fl oz lemon juice
2 fresh chillies, seeded (optional) and chopped
2 tablespoons dried parsley or 6 tablespoons chopped fresh parsley
½ teaspoon coarsely ground black pepper

Place the joint on a plate or platter to fit inside the refrigerator. Generously grind pepper over the meat.

Put the marinade ingredients in a food processor or blender and process them into a paste. Spread the paste over the meat, cover well with cling film, refrigerate and leave to season for 4–24 hours.

Heat the oven to 180C/350F/gas 4.

Transfer the joint to a greased roasting tin and roast for about 1½ hours for rare and 2 hours for medium meat. Serve with plain boiled rice and Cucumber raita (page 139).

North Indian beef and aubergine casserole

Shemali gaye ke tukre baygan-walla

Preparation and cooking time: 1 hour 45 minutes   Serves 4

900g/2lb boneless lean beef, chopped
275ml/12floz plain yoghurt
1/2 teaspoon salt
1/2 teaspoon freshly ground black pepper
5 tablespoons olive oil
1 small aubergine, sliced
8–9 small spring onions
1 green pepper, sliced
1 large tomato, sliced
4–5 dried red chillies, seeded (optional)

Heat the oven to 180C/375F/gas 5. Combine the beef, yoghurt, half of the salt and half of the pepper in a 1.1L/2pt soufflé or similar-sized ovenproof dish greased with two tablespoons of the olive oil.

Slice the aubergine and spread the slices on top of the beef.

For the next layer, cover with the spring onions, using only the bulbs plus 7.5–10cm/3–4in of the green stems.

For the next layers, spread the sliced green pepper, then the sliced tomato.

In a small bowl, mix together the rest of the yoghurt with the rest of the salt and pepper, and beat with a fork. Spread over to form the top layer.

Place the dried chillies on top and pour the rest of the olive oil over the whole dish.

Cover with a lid or foil and bake for 1½ hours. A substantial dish, serve it with a Raw spinach salad (page 176) or Chicory-walnut salad (page 173).

Royal kofta (meatballs)

Shahi kofta

Preparation and cooking time: 2½ hours   *Serves 8*

900 g/2 lb minced lean beef
275 ml/10 fl oz plain yoghurt
1½ teaspoons salt
2 teaspoons dried parsley or 2 tablespoons finely chopped fresh parsley
25 mm/1 in piece of fresh ginger root, cut into small pieces
5 green chillies, seeded (optional)
6 garlic cloves
4 tablespoons lemon juice
1½ teaspoons cayenne pepper
¼ teaspoon turmeric
¼ teaspoon ground coriander
3 medium-sized onions, peeled and chopped
225 ml/8 fl oz vegetable oil
6 bay leaves, crumbled
12 cloves
1 large pinch of saffron

Mix the minced beef, 50 ml/2 fl oz of the yoghurt, 1 teaspoon of the salt and the parsley together and set aside.

Combine the ginger, 3 of the chillies, garlic cloves and half the lemon juice in a food processor to make a paste.

Transfer the paste to a bowl and add the cayenne pepper, turmeric and ground coriander.

Place the meat mixture in a food processor and add the remaining lemon juice and 2 remaining chillies. Process until fairly fine.

From this mixture make balls, approximately 4 cm/1½ in in diameter.

Heat the oil in a large, thick-bottomed saucepan. Brown the onions over medium heat, stirring, then add bay leaves and cloves.

Add reserved paste to the hot browned onions, together with 275 ml/10 fl oz hot water and the rest of the salt, and cook for 10–15 minutes over a low heat. Add the rest of the yoghurt and cook for 5 more minutes.

Carefully add the meatballs to the sauce. They should be nearly submerged. Add the saffron.

Cover and cook slowly for 1½ hours. The meatballs should not break, but if some of them do, they will still taste fine. If you want to turn them use a wooden spoon and do so gently.

Serve with Basmati pillau (page 185) and Lemon lentils (page 192-3).

Cubed beef with spring onions and chillies

Hari piyaz aur mirch-walli boti

Preparation and cooking time: about 40 minutes   *Serves 4*

125 ml/4 fl oz vegetable oil
1 medium-sized onion, peeled and chopped
1.4 kg/3 lb boneless lean beef, cubed
2 teaspoons cumin seeds
225 ml/8 fl oz lemon juice
4 garlic cloves
2 whole fresh green chillies, seeded (optional)
¼ teaspoon salt
2 teaspoons freshly ground black pepper
12 spring onions, bulbs and 7.5 cm/3 in of the stem

Heat the oil in a large frying-pan over medium heat. When hot, add the onion and stir continually until it turns golden, about 4 minutes.

Add the beef and cumin seeds to the pan and cook for 15

minutes, stirring occasionally and lowering the heat if necessary to prevent burning.

Add the lemon juice, garlic, chillies, salt and pepper, and continue cooking for 10 minutes.

Add spring onions and cook another 10 minutes.

Serve with Lemon lentils (page 192-3) and warmed pitta bread.

Spicy beef potato cakes

Qeema aloo tikki

Preparation and cooking time: about 1 hour   *Serves 4*

25 mm/1 in fresh ginger root, peeled and chopped
4 garlic cloves, peeled and chopped
2 fresh green chillies, seeded (optional) and chopped
2 tablespoons dried parsley or 25 g/1 oz finely chopped fresh parsley
4 tablespoons lemon juice
½ teaspoon freshly ground black pepper
4 tablespoons vegetable oil
1 medium-sized onion, peeled and chopped
8 cloves
450 g/1 lb minced lean beef
3 large eggs
50 g/2 oz butter
For the potato patties
4 large potatoes, boiled
1 tablespoon vegetable oil
¼ teaspoon salt
1 teaspoon cayenne pepper
2 tablespoons cream

Place the ginger, garlic, chillies, parsley, lemon juice and pepper in a food processor or blender to make a 'loose' paste. Reserve the paste. (This *hara masala*, or fresh green mixture, may be used to cook meat or chicken dishes. It is a fine all-purpose, very useful flavouring mixture).

Heat the oil in a large frying-pan over medium-low heat. Add the onion and cloves to brown, stirring frequently.

Add the meat to the pan, stirring, to brown. After about 5 minutes, add the reserved *masala* paste. Cook over low heat for about 20 minutes or until the mixture is quite dry, stirring occasionally. Remove from the heat and reserve.

For the patties, peel the boiled potatoes, mash them with a fork, put them in a bowl and mix in the oil, salt, pepper and cream. With your hands, make round patties about 7.5 cm/3 in in diameter and 6 mm/¼ in thick or less. The potatoes have to be well mashed so they will make fairly thin patties. A food processor may do the job well, but mashing by hand has worked well for centuries.

Place a portion of the dry beef mixture on one patty, place another patty over it and pinch the edges together gently to join them, making a sort of meat-filled potato dumpling.

Beat the eggs together with a fork. Dip the patties into the beaten egg mixture to coat them, which also helps hold them together.

Melt the butter in a frying-pan over low heat. Add the patties and fry them about 3 minutes on each side, turning once, until nicely browned. Serve with Tomato mint raita (page 175) and warmed pitta bread.

Baked spicy beefburgers

Chapli kabab

This is my version of the hamburger. It is baked, rather than fried or grilled, and it is a bit spicier than the usual burger.

Preparation and cooking time: 40 minutes   *Serves 4–6*

700g/1½lb lean minced beef
4 tablespoons lemon juice
2 medium-sized eggs
1 teaspoon cayenne pepper
½ teaspoon salt
1 teaspoon parsley flakes or 1 tablespoon finely chopped fresh parsley
vegetable oil for greasing

Heat the oven to 230C/450F/gas 8. Mix all the ingredients together well and form the mixture into 4–6 patties.

Place them on a greased baking sheet and bake for 15–20 minutes.

Serve them with good mustard and bread.

Gingerburgers

Adrak-walla chapli kabab

Here's another version of my hamburger with a surprise element of ginger.

Preparation and cooking time: 15–25 minutes   *Serves 4–6*

700g/1½lb lean minced beef
2 medium-sized eggs
4 tablespoons plain yoghurt
25mm/1in fresh ginger root, grated
1 green chilli, seeded (optional) and finely chopped
¼ teaspoon salt
1–2 garlic cloves, peeled and finely chopped

Heat the grill to medium-high. Combine all the ingredients thoroughly. Form the mixture into 4–6 patties and place them on a grill pan or a baking sheet.

Place under grill, turning once, about 10 minutes for rare meat, about 15 minutes for medium, and about 18–20 minutes for well done. Serve with your favourite mustard and good bread.

The Chef/Film Producer Ismail Merchant at home in his kitchen in upstate New York.

Ingredients in Indian sweets are nuts, fruits and fresh milk or cream. Pictured are raisins, pistachios, cashews, almonds and walnuts.

A sampling of spices and seasonings. The 1st thali contains, clockwise from the top, coriander, mixed dried herbs, whole black pepper, cinnamon, cayenne pepper and turmeric, with parsley and cinnamon sticks in the centre. The 2nd thali contains, clockwise from the top, coriander, black cardamom pods, red chilli powder, cumin seeds, cardamom pods, coarse ground pepper and whole nutmegs, with nutmeg and cloves in the centre.

Verena Tarrant (Madeleine Potter) takes tea with Henry Burrage (John van Ness Philip) and Mr Gracie (Peter Bogyo) in *The Bostonians*.

The Nawab's banquet from *Heat and Dust*.

Indian/American summer picnic in Claverack, New York. Chicken tandoori is served with Coconut and mint chutney, Tarragon and walnut potato salad, a cool mango chutney and fresh cherries.

Winter's Sunday supper in the country consisting of poppadums, *Qeema* garnished with tomatoes, Caraway and onion potato salad, Beetroot vinaigrette and Spicy stewed cauliflower and potatoes.

Late night after theatre supper consisting of Spicy red cabbage, Basmati pillau, Lemon lentils and Chicken in coconut sauce.

Picnic in Claverack, featuring, anti-clockwise from the flowers, Cyrus Jhabvala, Diane Kagan, Richard Robbins, Ruth Jhabvala, Madhur Jaffrey, Sanford Allen, Ismail Merchant and James Ivory.

The Nawab's picnic from *Heat and Dust*.

James Mason and Madhur Jaffrey enjoy samosas, vanilla walnut cake and tea in *Autobiography of a Princess*.

An arrangement of the simple, basic ingredients in Ismail Merchant's cooking.

Mince with potatoes

Aloo qeema

Preparation and cooking time: about 50 minutes   *Serves 4*

4 tablespoons vegetable oil
3 medium-sized onions, peeled and chopped
1 cinnamon stick, broken up
900 g/2 lb minced lean beef
2 large potatoes, peeled and cut into bite-sized pieces
25 mm/1 in piece of fresh ginger root, grated
4 tablespoons plain yoghurt
1 large green chilli, seeded (optional) and chopped
½ teaspoon salt
2 medium-sized tomatoes, chopped

Heat the oil in a large frying-pan over medium heat and brown the onions with the cinnamon.

Add the meat and stir continually until it begins to brown, 4–5 minutes.

Add the potatoes, ginger, yoghurt, chilli, salt and tomatoes.

Cover and cook over low heat for a further 40 minutes or until the meat is tender. Serve with plain boiled rice and Green lentil dal (page 191).

* For mince with peas or spinach, follow the preceding recipe, but add 225 g/8 oz fresh shelled or frozen peas, or fresh trimmed or frozen spinach in place of, *or* in addition to, the potatoes in the last 5–7 minutes of cooking.

Mince with peas Kashmiri-style

Kashmiri qeema matter

Preparation and cooking time: 30–40 minutes   *Serves 2–3*

450 g/1 lb minced lean beef or lamb
salt ¼ teaspoon asafoetida
225 g/8 oz plain yoghurt, whisked
4 cm/1½ in fresh ginger root, grated
125 ml/4 fl oz vegetable oil
125 g/4 oz shelled peas, defrosted if frozen
1½ teaspoons chilli powder
1 teaspoon ground coriander
½ teaspoon ground allspice
handful of chopped coriander leaves

Mix the meat, salt to taste, asafoetida, yoghurt and ginger together.

Heat the oil in a large frying-pan over medium-low heat. Add the meat mixture, stirring occasionally to break up the meat.

When the mixture begins to dry out, add the peas, chilli powder, ground coriander, and allspice and cook until the meat is well browned, stirring continuously to prevent burning.

Add 225 ml/8 fl oz hot water, then gently simmer until the peas are cooked, about 10 minutes.

Remove the mixture from the pan with a slotted spoon, transfer to a serving dish and stir in the coriander leaves. Serve with Cashew rice (page 187) and Cucumber raita (page 139).

Spicy minced beef kebabs

Motlabai sheekh kabab

Preparation and cooking time: about 20 minutes   *Serves 4*

2 tablespoons butter
1 large onion, peeled and chopped
3 garlic cloves, peeled and chopped
25 mm/1 in fresh ginger root, chopped
1 teaspoon ground cumin
½ teaspoon ground cardamom
450 g/1 lb boneless lean minced beef, lamb or pork
3½ tablespoons dry breadcrumbs
1 beaten egg
3 tablespoons chopped mint leaves
1 green chilli, seeded (optional) and chopped
4 tablespoons lemon juice
1 teaspoon salt
½ teaspoon cayenne pepper
½ teaspoon freshly ground black pepper
about 425 ml/15 fl oz vegetable oil

Heat the butter in a frying-pan over low heat. Add the onion and sauté for three minutes. Add the garlic, ginger, cumin and cardamom, sauté the mixture, stirring occasionally, another 3–4 minutes, and reserve.

Mix together the meat, breadcrumbs, egg, mint, chilli, lemon juice, salt, cayenne and black pepper.

Add the fried onion mixture to the meat mixture and shape into patties about 5 cm/2 in in diameter.

Heat the oil, about 20 mm/¾ in deep, in a deep frying-pan over medium heat. Add the patties 2 or 3 at a time to give the oil time to reheat and cook until the patties are well browned, turning them frequently. Drain them on kitchen paper and serve with a mixed salad and warmed pitta bread.

Cubed beef

Gayki boti

Preparation and cooking time: 45 minutes   *Serves 4*

1.4 kg/3 lb stewing beef, cubed
3 medium-sized onions, peeled and chopped
4 garlic cloves, peeled and chopped
4 tablespoons lemon juice
2 teaspoon Dijon mustard
1 teaspoon salt
125 ml/4 fl oz vegetable oil

Heat the oven to 200C/400F/gas 6.

Combine all the ingredients with 125 ml/4 fl oz water in a heavy casserole or ovenproof dish and bake for 40 minutes.

Serve with Raw spinach salad (page 176) and warmed pitta bread.

Roast ginger beef
Bhuna adrak-walla gosht

Preparation and cooking time: about 1 hour 20 minutes   *Serves 4*

1.6 kg/3½ lb sirloin joint
vegetable oil for greasing
25 g/1 oz chopped fresh parsley
5 cm/2 in fresh ginger root, peeled and grated
2 green chillies, seeded (optional) and chopped
2 tablespoons Dijon mustard
2 tablespoons lemon juice
¼ teaspoon salt

Heat the oven to 150C/300F/gas 2. Place the beef in greased baking tin, fat side up.

Combine the parsley, ginger, chillies, mustard, lemon juice and salt in a food processor or blender.

Rub the mixture all over the meat. Cover the meat very well with the mixture.

Bake about 1 hour 10 minutes for medium-rare meat, a little longer for medium. Serve with warmed pitta bread and Lemon lentils (page 192-3).

Lamb and cashew stew

Kaju gosht

Preparation and cooking time: 1¼–1½ hours   *Serves 5–6*

900g/2 lb boneless lean lamb, cut in large bite-sized pieces
8 medium-sized onions, peeled and finely chopped
8 tablespoons vegetable oil
½ tablespoon salt
8 cloves
8 peppercorns
3 cinnamon sticks
1 tablespoon caraway seeds
1 tablespoon cumin seeds
4–5 bay leaves
225 ml/8 fl oz plain yoghurt
8–10 garlic cloves, peeled and crushed
3 tablespoons coriander leaves, finely chopped
For the chilli paste
10–15 green chillies, seeded
6 mm/¼ in fresh ginger root
6 garlic cloves, peeled
For the cashew paste
100g/4 oz cashews
3 tablespoons sesame seeds
3 tablespoons poppy seeds

Heat half the oil in a large saucepan over high heat. When hot, add the lamb and cook, stirring frequently, until it is browned on all sides, about 5 minutes.

Remove the lamb from the pan with a slotted spoon and reserve. Turn the heat to medium, add the rest of the oil and the onions, and cook, stirring frequently, until the onions soften, 7–8 minutes.

Return the lamb to the pan with the salt, spices and hot water to cover. Bring to the boil, then simmer for 25 minutes or until the meat is cooked but not tender. Drain and reserve the water and return the mixture to the pan.

Meanwhile, make the chilli paste by processing the chillies, ginger root and garlic to a paste in a food processor or in batches in a blender and reserve. For the cashew paste, purée the nuts and seeds similarly and reserve.

Add the chilli paste and gently simmer the mixture over low heat for 10–15 minutes, adding a few tablespoonfuls of the reserved stock as necessary to prevent burning.

Add the cashew paste and simmer for another 10–15 minutes, adding stock as necessary.

Add the yoghurt and let it simmer for 5 minutes.

Add stock according to the thickness of sauce you desire. Simmer gently until the meat is tender, adding a little more stock as necessary.

Heat the rest of the oil in a small saucepan over medium-low heat and add the garlic. When the garlic is golden, add it to the stew with the chopped coriander, cover immediately and cook gently for 5 more minutes. Uncover just before serving. Serve with Saffron pillau (page 183).

Spiced Kashmiri lamb

Kashmiri gosht

Preparation and cooking time: 1¼ hours   *Serves 4*

450g/1 lb boneless lean lamb, cut in large bite-sized pieces
2 large onions, peeled and sliced
425 ml/15 fl oz yoghurt, beaten
3 tablespoons vegetable oil
1 tablespoon poppy seeds
½ teaspoon salt
150g/5 oz slivered almonds
¾ tablespoon chilli powder
¼ teaspoon powdered saffron

Put the lamb, onions, yoghurt and oil into a saucepan and mix well. Bring the mixture to a boil, lower the heat and simmer gently, uncovered, until the meat is tender, about 45 minutes, adding a little hot water at a time as necessary.

Grind the poppy seeds in a pestle and mortar, an electric coffee mill or food processor or blender until they form a paste. Add the salt, poppy seed paste and almonds to the saucepan, stirring them in well, and continue cooking until the mixture is dry.

Stir in the chilli powder and saffron and let the mixture cook, almost frying, for 5 minutes. Serve hot with Basmati pillau (page 185) and a mixed salad.

Minced lamb kebab

Gosht kabab

Preparation and cooking time: *Serves 6*
  boiling the potatoes, plus 20–25 minutes

1.3 kg/2 lb boneless lamb shoulder, cut in large dice
4 cm/1½ in fresh ginger root, peeled and cut into 3–4 pieces
2 large potatoes, boiled, peeled and chopped
3 green chillies, seeded (optional) and chopped
125 ml/4 fl oz plain yoghurt
½ teaspoon salt
1 teaspoon black pepper
1 tablespoon vegetable oil, for greasing

Heat the grill to high. Place the lamb, ginger, potatoes, chillies, yoghurt, salt and pepper in a food processor. Process for about 30 seconds (pulsing as it goes to keep the mixture moving properly) or until the mixture is a coarse purée.

Form the mixture into 6–8 patties, about 7.5 cm/3 in in diameter, and place them flat on a greased roasting tin.

Place the tin 20–22.5 cm/4–5 in under the grill and cook the kebabs for 12–15 minutes, turning once, for medium meat, or longer if wished.

Serve the kebabs with pitta bread and a fresh salad.

* You can also fry these kebabs in a lightly greased pan, though I prefer them grilled.

Roast veal with mustard and ginger
Rai adrak-walla bachra

Preparation and cooking time: *Serves 4–6*
  5 hours marinating, plus 2 hours 10 minutes

2 tablespoons vegetable oil
2.7 kg/6 lb loin of veal, boned and rolled
1 teaspoon cayenne pepper
2 tablespoons Dijon mustard (preferably flavoured with green pepper-
  corns)
125 ml/4 fl oz lemon juice
1 teaspoon salt, plus extra for sprinkling
7.5 cm/3 in fresh ginger root, peeled and grated
2 tablespoons parsley flakes or 25 g/1 oz fresh parsley, finely chopped

Coat a roasting tin with the oil and place the veal in the tin.

Mix together the cayenne pepper, mustard, lemon juice and salt, and pour this over the veal.

Top the mixture with the ginger, parsley and a sprinkling of salt, and leave the meat to season in the refrigerator for 5 hours.

Heat the oven to 180C/350F/gas 4 and when hot bake the meat for 2 hours. Serve with Savoury onion rice (page 184).

* If you have time, the meat will be more tender when roasted for 3 hours at 150C/300F/gas 2.

Vegetables

Nul Bazaar was only a few hundred steps from the house where I grew up in Bombay. With six sisters, visiting uncles, aunts, nephews and nieces, there was always a great deal of shopping to be done. The bazaar was the centre of great activity of all kinds, but the main one for us was buying food — everything from fresh vegetables and fruit to meat, fish, chicken, pulses and spices.

My father and I would proceed from stall to stall and look for the very best quality at the best price. 'You get what you pay for, sir,' one vegetable vendor would respond to my father's comments. She was very prosperous looking, the weight of her gold earrings stretching her ear lobes, and had a bright red 'bindi' in the centre of her forehead. As she sprinkled water on her piles of vegetables to keep them crisp and fresh looking, she seemed always ready for a fight. But she enjoyed a laugh, too, and I looked forward to seeing her.

In the bazaar the day's produce was collected fresh from farmers and sold the same day. Selling began at 6.30 in the morning and by 11 a.m. all the fresh vegetables were gone. The fruit sellers' stalls would be open all day, but the shopkeepers would nap between 1 and 4 in the afternoon, covering their stalls with gunnysacks. After napping, they would roll up the gunnysacks and the marvellously coloured fruit would re-appear.

The bounty laid out before us in the bazaar was wonderful. We could touch the live poultry, smell the melons, squeeze the vegetables and fruit. In fact, we were encouraged to do so. It was an important part of shopping in the bazaar and taught me one of a cook's most important — and obvious — lessons: choose the freshest and most beautiful fruits and vegetables.

Alas, when I came to America as a young man I saw everything in the supermarkets wrapped in cellophane. Touching and smelling and examining too closely are frowned upon and discouraged, so participation by the shopper and the entire shopping experience is diminished. This is still true of most markets, I'm afraid, but there are some wonderful new markets for fruit and vegetables appearing in the West which are more in the style of the Orient. There is little cellophane or plastic in evidence, and one is free to touch, smell and select the most appealing fruit and vegetables. We should all definitely patronize these markets.

Boiled potatoes with spring onions and chives

Aloo aur hari piyaz ki sabzi

Preparation and cooking time: 10–15 minutes   *Serves 4*

700g/1½lb small potatoes
6 tablespoons snipped chives
3 spring onions, chopped
4 garlic cloves, peeled and chopped
50g/2oz butter
2 sage leaves, chopped
½ green chilli, seeded (optional) and chopped
salt

Boil the potatoes in their jackets until they are just tender, then drain and cut up each one into 2–3 pieces.

While the potatoes are still hot, add the chives, onions, garlic, butter, sage, chilli and salt to taste. Serve hot.

Potatoes and peas

Aloo mattar

Preparation and cooking time: 30 minutes   *Serves 6–8*

8 medium-sized potatoes
125 ml/4 fl oz vegetable oil
1 medium-sized onion, peeled and sliced
2 teaspoons cumin seeds
1 teaspoon freshly ground black pepper
2 medium-sized tomatoes, sliced
450 g/1 lb fresh shelled or frozen and defrosted green peas
salt

Peel and slice the potatoes and reserve.

Heat the oil in a frying-pan over medium-low heat. When hot, add the onion and cook until it begins to brown, stirring occasionally.

Add the potatoes and cook for 10 minutes over medium heat, stirring occasionally.

Add the cumin, pepper, tomatoes, peas and salt to taste. Continue cooking, stirring occasionally, until the potatoes are crisp, 10–15 minutes.

Va-va-voom potatoes

Khas aloo

This dish is so good you'll be glad of any leftovers.

Preparation and cooking time: about 15 minutes   Serves 6

1.1 kg/2½ lb small red potatoes
125 g/4 oz tarragon vinegar
4 tablespoons walnut oil
8 dried red peppers, seeded (optional)
1 teaspoon mustard seeds
1 teaspoon salt
1½ teaspoons dill weed

Boil the potatoes in their jackets. Do not overcook them; they should be just firm.

Combine the vinegar, oil, peppers, mustard seeds, salt and dill weed in a saucepan.

Drain and halve the unskinned potatoes, mix them with the other ingredients and cook for 10 minutes, covered, over low heat. Serve hot.

Sautéed mushrooms
Kumbhi khas

Preparation and cooking time: 10 minutes   *Serves 4–6*

75 g/3 oz butter
3 tablespoons lemon juice
½ teaspoon cayenne pepper
½ teaspoon cumin seeds
175 g/6 oz button mushrooms, cleaned and sliced

Melt the butter in a frying-pan over low heat and add the lemon juice, cayenne pepper and cumin seeds. Cook for 3–4 minutes.

Add the mushrooms and sauté for 5–6 minutes.

Mushrooms sautéed in mustard oil
Rai-walli kumbhi

Preparation and cooking time: about 5 minutes   *Serves 3–4*

3 tablespoons mustard oil
4 tablespoons lemon juice
4 bay leaves, crumbled
1 teaspoon chilli powder
12 medium-sized button mushrooms, sliced

Heat the oil in a saucepan over low heat. Add the lemon juice, bay leaves and chilli powder, and cook for 1 minute.

Add the mushrooms and cook for 3–4 minutes only. The mushrooms should not be overcooked.

Cucumber raita

Kheera ka raita

Preparation time: 5 minutes, plus chilling *Serves 5–6*

425 ml/15 fl oz plain yoghurt
1 medium-sized cucumber, grated
½ teaspoon salt
½ teaspoon ground cumin
sprig of mint, chopped

Stir the yoghurt with a fork until it is smooth.

Grate the cucumber and stir it into the yoghurt with the salt, cumin and mint. Chill slightly before serving.

Spicy vegetarian curry

Masaledar sabzi

Preparation and cooking time: *Serves 4*
  making the tamarind water, plus 35 minutes

4 large potatoes, peeled and coarsely chopped
salt
¼ teaspoon turmeric
3 medium-sized tomatoes, blanched, skinned and mashed
125 ml/4 fl oz thick tamarind water (see below)
2 tablespoons dark brown sugar (jaggery)
For the masala
3 tablespoons vegetable oil
1 medium-sized onion, peeled and finely chopped
25 mm/1 in fresh ginger root
1–2 garlic cloves, peeled and pressed or finely chopped
2 teaspoons chilli powder
2 tablespoons desiccated coconut
1 teaspoon cumin seeds
1 tablespoon sesame seeds
1 tablespoon poppy seeds

First make the *masala*. Heat the oil in a saucepan over medium-low heat. When hot, add the onion, and cook, stirring occasionally until it softens.

Add the rest of the *masala* ingredients to the pan, and cook, stirring occasionally, for 3–4 minutes or until the mixture becomes reddish.

Add the potatoes, and cook over medium heat, stirring frequently, for 3–4 minutes.

Add 850 ml/1½ pt hot water, salt and the turmeric to the pan, and simmer until the potatoes are just cooked.

Add the tomatoes, tamarind water and sugar. Boil until the jaggery dissolves. Serve with plain boiled rice.

* To make tamarind water, soak a small lump of tamarind in warm water for 15–20 minutes. Squeeze the tamarind with your fingers, then strain off the tamarind water.

Spicy potatoes, cauliflower and peas
Aloo phoolgobi mattar ki sabzi

Preparation and cooking time: about 25 minutes   *Serves 6–8*

4 tablespoons vegetable oil
2 medium-sized onions, peeled and chopped
2 large garlic cloves, peeled and chopped
2 green chillies, seeded (optional) and chopped
¼ teaspoon turmeric
½ teaspoon cayenne pepper
12 black peppercorns
6 meduim-sized potatoes
1 medium-sized cauliflower, halved, cored and cut into large florets
½ teaspoon salt
4 tablespoons lemon juice

Heat the oil in a large deep saucepan over low heat. When hot, add the onions, garlic, chillies, turmeric, cayenne pepper and peppercorns. Cook the mixture 10 minutes, stirring occasionally.

Peel the potatoes and cut them into thick slices, then stir them into the mixture. Add the cauliflower florets and stir them in, too.

Add the salt, lemon juice and 225 ml/8 fl oz hot water. Continue cooking over low heat for about 25 minutes, adding the peas during the last 10 minutes of cooking.

N.B. The vegetables should be tender, but do not overcook them.

Merchant's spinach purée

Palak bharta

Preparation and cooking time: Serves 2
   preparing the spinach, plus 10 minutes

800g/1½lb spinach, washed and trimmed, or 225g/8oz spinach,
   defrosted if frozen
2 spring onions
1 tablespoon butter
½ teaspoon salt
1 tablespoon Dijon mustard

Add the spinach to a pan of boiling water and cook, stirring occasionally, until it is tender, 1–3 minutes.

Drain the spinach through a colander, pressing the greens with the back of a spoon to get rid of excess moisture.

Place the spinach, spring onions, butter, salt and mustard into a food processor. Purée the mixture and serve hot.

Spinach Jannu

Palak Jannu

Preparation and cooking time: *Serves 2–3*
   preparing the spinach, plus 10 minutes

800g/1½lb spinach, washed and trimmed, or 225g/8oz frozen
   spinach, defrosted
1 medium-sized onion, peeled and chopped
1–2 garlic cloves
juice of ½ lemon
1 tablespoon Dijon mustard
pinch of salt
¼ teaspoon freshly ground black pepper
50g/2oz butter

Add the spinach to a pan of boiling water and cook, stirring occasionally, until it is tender, 1–3 minutes.

Drain the spinach through a colander, pressing the greens with the back of a spoon to get rid of excess moisture.

Place the spinach in a food processor or blender with the onion, garlic, lemon juice, mustard, salt, pepper and butter. Purée the mixture and serve hot.

Stuffed potato patties

Aloo tikki

Preparation and cooking time: *Serves 4*
  boiling the potatoes, plus about 25 minutes

4 large potatoes, boiled in their jackets until very tender
1 tablespoon vegetable oil
¼ teaspoon salt
1 teaspoon cayenne pepper
2 tablespoons cream
3 large eggs
about 50g/2oz butter
For the pea stuffing
225g/8oz green peas, defrosted if frozen
¼ teaspoon fresh green chilli, seeded (optional) and chopped
25g/1oz chopped fresh parsley
For the spinach stuffing
225g/8oz spinach, washed and trimmed, or 75g/3oz frozen spinach,
  defrosted
1–2 green chillies, seeded (optional) and chopped
pinch of salt
¼ teaspoon freshly ground black pepper

First make one of the stuffings. For the pea stuffing, cook the peas in boiling water until done and drain them through a colander. Stir in the chilli and parsley.

For the spinach stuffing, cook the spinach in boiling water until done and drain it through a colander. Stir in the chillies, salt and pepper.

To make the patties, peel the boiled potatoes, then mash them with the oil, salt, pepper and cream.

With your hands, make round patties about 7cm/3in in diameter and 6mm/¼in thick. The potato mixture has to be well mashed to make fairly thin patties. A food processor does this job beautifully.

Place a portion of spinach or pea filling on one patty, place another patty over it and pinch the edges together gently to seal them.

Beat the eggs together with a fork. Dip the patties into the beaten egg mixture. This helps hold them together and also gives them a nice crust.

Heat 50g/2oz butter in a large frying-pan over medium-low heat. When hot, carefully add the patties, without overlapping them, and cook about 6 minutes, turning once, or until they are nicely browned. Serve right away.

Sautéed courgettes
Tali gilki

Preparation and cooking time: 10 minutes   *Serves 4*

3–4 medium-sized courgettes
25g/1oz butter
4 tablespoons lemon juice
4 sage leaves, chopped, or ½ teaspoon dried sage
¼ teaspoon freshly ground black pepper
¼ teaspoon salt

Cut the courgettes into 3mm/⅛in slices, discarding the very ends.

Melt the butter in a deep frying-pan over medium-low heat. When hot, stir in the courgettes and the rest of the ingredients, and cook, stirring frequently, until the courgettes are barely tender. Serve immediately.

Potato 'chaat'

Aloo chaat

Leftover boiled potatoes and French beans are fine for this dish. *Chaat* in Hindi means 'something that excites the palate'.

Preparation and cooking time: *Serves 4*
    boiling the potatoes and beans, plus about 10 minutes

40–40g/1½–2oz butter
450g/1 lb potatoes, boiled
pinch of salt
1 tablespoon Dijon mustard
125g/4oz French beans, cooked
1 tablespoon chopped fresh parsley

Melt the butter in a frying-pan over medium-low heat. Add the potatoes, salt, mustard and beans, if using, and stir.

Cook the mixture for about 10 minutes or until it is thoroughly hot. Sprinkle the parsley over it and serve immediately.

Fried vegetable toast

Sabzi-walla toast

Preparation and cooking time: 50 minutes   *Serves 6–8*

100g/3½oz carrots, chopped
200g/7oz green cabbage, chopped
200g/7oz shelled peas, defrosted if frozen
3 large potatoes, peeled
4 tablespoons cornflour
6 coriander leaves, chopped
juice of 2 lemons
8–10 green chillies, seeded (optional) and finely chopped
salt
12 slices of white bread
vegetable oil for frying
tomato chutney, to serve (page 220)

Cook the carrots and cabbage in boiling salted water until they are almost tender. Add the peas and continue cooking until all are tender.

Drain, then mash the vegetables.

Meanwhile boil the potatoes until tender, then mash them.

Add the potatoes to the mashed vegetables with the cornflour, coriander leaves, juice of lemons, chillies, and salt to taste, mixing well. Mix in more cornflour, if necessary, to make a fairly stiff paste.

Cut the bread slices into halves and spread a thick layer of vegetable mixture over them.

Heat about 25mm/1in oil in a large frying-pan over medium-low heat. When hot, fry the slices, a few at a time, with the mixture face down for about 4–5 minutes or until the mixture begins to brown.

Serve the vegetable toasts hot with Tomato chutney (page 220).

Clove garlic mixed vegetables

Ganga Jumna subzi

The Gunga and the Jumna are two holy rivers in India which give their name to this quite heavenly mixture.

Preparation and cooking time: about 40 minutes   Serves 6

6 medium-sized carrots, peeled and sliced
2 medium-sized potatoes, peeled and sliced
225g/8oz shelled green peas, defrosted if frozen
225g/8oz green beans, topped and tailed, defrosted if frozen
4 medium-sized beetroot
3 medium-sized tomatoes
125ml/4floz vegetable oil
2 medium-sized onions, peeled and chopped
4 bay leaves, crumbled
12 cloves
6 garlic cloves
½ tablespoon chilli powder

Chop and combine the carrots, potatoes, peas, beans, beetroot and tomatoes in a bowl and reserve.

Heat the oil in a saucepan over medium-low heat and add the onions, bay leaves and cloves. Cook them for 5–6 minutes, stirring occasionally.

Add the garlic and chilli powder and continue cooking for 5–6 minutes.

Add the reserved vegetables and cook for 15 minutes or until vegetables are tender. Do not overcook them and serve hot.

Cayenned corn

Makai ke dane mirch-walli

Preparation and cooking time: 15 minutes   *Serves 4*

4–5 corn on the cob
40g/1½oz butter
125ml/4floz light cream
2 garlic cloves, peeled and chopped
pinch of salt
½ teaspoon cayenne pepper

Cut the raw kernels away from the cobs with a sharp knife.

Melt the butter in a frying pan over low heat. Add the corn, then the cream, garlic, salt and pepper.

Simmer gently for 8–10 minutes until the corn is tender. Serve right away.

Stewed cauliflower and tomatoes

Gobi tamatar

Preparation and cooking time: 35–40 minutes   *Serves 4*

75 ml/3 fl oz vegetable oil
½ medium-sized onion, peeled and chopped
3 bay leaves, crumbled
1 medium-sized cauliflower, cleaned and cut into small florets
2 medium-sized tomatoes, chopped
4 tablespoons vinegar
½ teaspoon salt
½ teaspoon cayenne pepper
juice of ½ lemon

Heat the oil in a saucepan over medium-low heat. Add the onion and cook until it begins to brown.

Add the bay leaves and cauliflower, then the tomatoes, vinegar, salt, pepper and lemon juice. Cover and cook for 30 minutes over low heat or until the cauliflower is tender.

Spicy stewed cauliflower and potatoes

Masaledar gobi aloo

Preparation and cooking time: 45–50 minutes   *Serves 4–6*

4 tablespoons vegetable oil
1 medium-sized onion, peeled and chopped
2 large potatoes, peeled and cut into small pieces
1 teaspoon cayenne pepper
4 tablespoons lemon juice
1 teaspoon salt
¼ teaspoon turmeric
1 medium-sized heart of cauliflower, washed and cut into medium-sized florets
1 green chilli, seeded (optional) and sliced
1 dried red chilli, seeded (optional) and crushed
125 ml/4 fl oz plain yoghurt mixed with 50 ml/2 fl oz water

Heat the oil in a large saucepan over medium-low heat. Add the onion, and cook until it begins to turn brown, stirring occasionally.

Stir in the pieces of potatoes and cook until they also begin to brown, stirring frequently.

Add the cayenne pepper, lemon, salt and turmeric, and cook over medium-low flame 2–3 minutes, stirring occasionally.

Add the cauliflower, green and red chillies and the yoghurt-water mixture, and stir well.

Continue cooking until the mixture is tender, 20–30 minutes.

Richard's cinnamon-dill carrots

Darchini aur suwa-walla gajar

Preparation and cooking time: 20 minutes   *Serves 6*

6 large carrots (1 per person)
25 g/1 oz butter
½ teaspoon ground cinnamon
1 tablespoon honey
pinch of salt
½ teaspoon coarsely ground peppercorns
½ tablespoon chopped dill

Peel the carrots and cut them into 5–7.5 cm/2–3 in long batons, uniformly slender.

Boil the carrots until tender but still firm, about 5 minutes.

Pour off the water. Add the butter to the pan and cook over very low heat for 2–3 minutes. Stir in the cinnamon, honey, salt and pepper and dill and serve right away.

Spicy red cabbage

Masaledar lal karam kalle

Preparation and cooking time: 35–45 minutes   *Serves 6–8*

4 tablespoons vegetable oil
2 medium-sized onions, peeled and chopped
1 tablespoon cumin seeds
1 tablespoon chilli powder
3 garlic cloves, peeled and finely chopped
900g–1.1kg/2–2½lb red cabbage, cored and sliced
1 teaspoon salt
4 tablespoons tarragon vinegar

Heat the oil in a saucepan over medium-low heat. When hot, add the onions, and cook, stirring occasionally, until they turn golden-brown.

Stir in the cumin seeds, chilli powder and garlic, and let the mixture cook over low heat for 10 minutes.

Add the cabbage and mix well. Add the salt, then add the vinegar, and cover. Cook for 20–30 minutes over low heat until the cabbage is very soft.

Sautéed red cabbage and raisins

Kismishi lal karem kalle

Preparation and cooking time: about 15 minutes   *Serves 4–6*

75 ml/3 fl oz vegetable oil
1 medium-sized onion, peeled and chopped
450 g/1 lb red cabbage, cored and finely chopped
¼ teaspoon cumin seeds
6 cloves
½ teaspoon salt
¼ teaspoon chilli powder
1 apple, cored and sliced with skin
4 tablespoons lemon juice
about 12 raisins

Heat the oil in a small saucepan over medium-low heat. When hot, add the onion and cook until the onion begins to brown, stirring occasionally.

Add the rest of the ingredients to the pan, and cook over low heat for 10 minutes, stirring occasionally, or until the cabbage is tender.

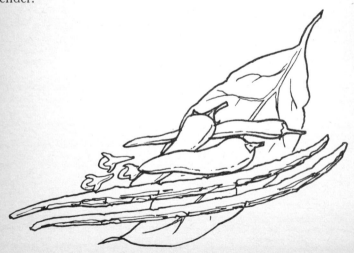

Broccoli in garlic-lemon butter

Nimbu aur lasson-walli broccoli

Preparation and cooking time: about 10 minutes   *Serves 3–4*

450 g/1 lb broccoli
75 g/3 oz butter
1 teaspoon chilli powder
4 garlic cloves, peeled and chopped
juice of 2 medium-sized lemons
1 teaspoon cumin seeds

Discard any thick, coarse ends, and steam or boil the broccoli for 8–10 minutes or until just tender. Be careful not to overcook so it remains green and slightly crisp.

Meanwhile, melt the butter in a saucepan with the rest of the ingredients over low heat.

Pour the garlic-lemon butter over the broccoli and serve.

Green beans in mustard sauce

Frazbeen sarsoon ke tail-walli

Preparation and cooking time: 20 minutes   *Serves 4–6*

450 g/1 lb green beans
1 tablespoon Dijon or Dusseldorf mustard
salt and freshly ground black pepper
1–1½ tablespoons lemon juice
4 tablespoons olive oil

Top and tail the beans, but leave them whole. Soak them in very cold water for 5–6 minutes.

Drain the beans and steam them in a vegetable steamer for about 5 minutes or until just tender. Alternatively, cook them in boiling water for 5 minutes. The important thing is not to overcook them.

Meanwhile, spoon the mustard into a small bowl and add the salt, pepper and lemon juice. Stir to blend, then whisk in the oil.

Drain the beans. Add the mustard sauce to them, toss to coat well and serve immediately.

Stewed aubergine

Baygan ka bharta

Preparation and cooking time: 25–30 minutes   *Serves 4*

4 tablespoons vegetable oil
1 medium-sized onion, peeled and chopped
4 bay leaves, crumbled
1 large aubergine, peeled and sliced
½ teaspoon chilli powder
½ teaspoon salt
425 g/15 oz canned tomatoes including juices
2 tablespoons red wine vinegar
½ teaspoon caraway seeds
75 ml/3 fl oz lemon juice

Heat the oil in a frying-pan over medium-low heat, add the onion and bay leaves and cook them for 4–5 minutes, stirring occasionally.

Meanwhile, peel the aubergine, slice it, then cut it into pieces. Add them and the rest of the ingredients to the pan.

Raise the heat until the mixture begins to simmer, then cover, reduce the heat and simmer for 20 minutes or until the aubergine is very tender.

Fresh asparagus in mustard dressing
Sarsoon-walli asparagus

Preparation and cooking time: about 10 minutes   Serves 4

20 asparagus sticks
2 tablespoons Dijon mustard
2 tablespoons tarragon vinegar
¼ teaspoon salt
¼ teaspoon cayenne pepper

Steam the asparagus until tender, about 10 minutes.

Meanwhile, whisk together the mustard, tarragon vinegar, salt and cayenne pepper.

Drain the asparagus, if necessary, and place it on a warmed serving platter. Pour the mustard sauce over the asparagus and serve.

Spiced okra
Masala bhindi

Preparation and cooking time: 20 minutes   Serves 4–6

1 tablespoon ground cumin
½ teaspoon turmeric
1 teaspoon chilli powder
¼ teaspoon salt
4 tablespoons lemon juice
1 teaspoon Dijon mustard
225g/8oz okra (about 30 small pods)
4 tablespoons vegetable oil

Mix the cumin, turmeric, chilli powder, salt and lemon juice in a small bowl.

Add the mustard and mix to make a rather wet paste.

Cut the stems off the okra pods. Then split them ¾ the way down. Split them again, dividing the pods into 4 equal parts which are held together by the narrow end tip.

Pour a little of the paste into the openings, and spread it lightly over all the pods but the narrow tip. Sprinkle with salt.

Heat the oil in a small frying-pan over low heat and fry the pods, covered, until they are tender, about 10 minutes, turning them once.

'Fasting Day' potatoes

Aftari aloo

This is a celebratory dish I created after a day of fasting.

Preparation and cooking time: about 20 minutes　　　*Serves 3–4*

4 medium-sized potatoes
75 ml/3 fl oz vegetable oil
1 medium-sized onion, peeled and diced
12 black peppercorns
½ teaspoon cumin seeds
3 garlic cloves, peeled and chopped
pinch of salt
4 tablespoons lemon juice
1 bunch fresh dill, stems discarded and chopped

Peel and slice the potatoes.

Heat the oil in a frying-pan over medium-low heat. When hot, add the onion, and cook until it begins to brown, stirring occasionally.

Add the peppercorns, cumin and garlic to the pan with the potatoes, salt, lemon juice and dill. Cook for about 15 minutes, stirring occasionally, or until the potatoes are tender. Serve hot.

Grilled courgettes with cumin butter
Zeera mukhon-walli gilki

Preparation and cooking time: 10 minutes   *Serves 6*

6 medium-sized courgettes
For the cumin butter
½ tablespoon chilli powder
40g/1½oz butter
¼ teaspoon salt
4–6 garlic cloves
1 teaspoon cumin seeds, bruised in a pestle and mortar

Heat the grill to high. Stir the cumin butter ingredients together in a bowl.

Slice the courgettes into halves lengthways and spread the butter over them.

Place them on a baking tin 10–12.5 cm/4–5 in under the grill, and cook for 8 minutes, or until just tender.

Coconut dumplings and vegetable stew

Dhokle

This is one of the great Indian dishes.

Preparation and cooking time: Serves 6
   12 hours soaking the chick peas, plus preparing the
   coconut, then 1½ hours

125 g/4 oz kabli channa (chick peas), picked over and washed
125 g/4 oz kala channa (brown chick peas), picked over and washed
225 ml/8 fl oz vegetable oil
1 medium-sized onion, peeled and chopped
6 bay leaves, crumbled
125 g/4 oz cauliflower, cut into small florets
125 g/4 oz French beans, topped and tailed
125 g/4 oz green peas
125 g/4 oz bobby beans, topped and tailed
125 g/4 oz green or red pepper
225 g/8 oz tomatoes
225 g/8 oz chick pea (gram) flour
225 g/8 oz millet flour
125 g/4 oz rice flour
3 tablespoons vegetable oil
2 tablespoons clarified butter
2 teaspoons ground coriander
½ teaspoon turmeric
about 1 teaspoon chilli powder
meat of ½ large coconut, grated
salt
225 g/8 oz potatoes, cut in large dice
125 g/4 oz aubergine, cut in large dice
For the green spice paste
6–8 green chillies, seeded (optional)
2 whole garlic pods, peeled and chopped
25 mm/1 in fresh ginger root, grated
1 tablespoon cumin seeds

Cover the yellow and brown chick peas with plenty of cold water and leave them to soak for 12 hours. Drain well.

Pound the ingredients for the green spice paste in a pestle and mortar, or purée them in a food processor or in batches in a blender, and reserve.

Heat the oil in a large saucepan. When hot, add the onion and bay leaves, and cook over medium-low heat, stirring occasionally, until the onion is light brown.

Add the cauliflower, French beans, peas, drained pulses, bobby beans and pepper to the onion. Cook for 15 minutes, stirring occasionally, then add ¾ of the green spice paste, stirring.

Chop the tomatoes, stir them into the saucepan, and cook for 5 minutes.

Add 1.1 L/2 pt hot water to the pan and continue cooking.

Meanwhile, mix the three flours in a soup plate and add the oil and clarified butter. Add the remaining green spice paste, the coriander, turmeric and chilli powder, ¾ of the grated coconut and stir to taste. Reserve the remaining grated coconut. (Keep the rest of the coconut meat for another dish.)

Stir the flour mixture to make a medium firm dough, adding a little water if necessary.

Form the dough into long, flat, smallish fist-shaped dumplings. When the vegetable mixture begins to boil, add the dumplings, potatoes, the rest of the grated coconut and the aubergine. Simmer the mixture over low heat for 30–40 minutes. Serve with plain boiled rice.

Salads

I include several of my favourite salads here. There is no 'cooking' as such in them, unless you actually boil the beetroots, as salads are best slightly chilled and crisp. Then they are cool and refreshing. This means that all the ingredients should be washed and carefully dried: water makes a salad soggy.

One of the very best and simplest salads is simply a great lettuce, properly washed and dried, then chilled, and dressed with a superior olive oil, a little salt and fresh lemon juice. It never fails. Don't forget to toss it, or any mixed or dressed salad, thoroughly. Most people stint on the tossing. Tossing is part of the ritual of salad making and should not be neglected under any circumstances.

If you're fortunate enough to have your own garden, even a small one, you will be immensely rewarded. There is absolutely nothing like salad ingredients taken straight from the garden to the salad bowl. I have had a garden for years, which I tend with my friend Dick Robbins in a rather haphazard way because of our busy schedules. But it rewards me, despite neglect.

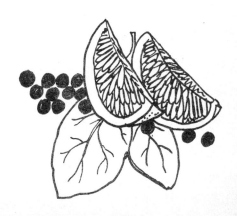

Green lentil salad

Haridal ka salaad

This original salad is made with 'leftovers' from my *Moong dal* recipe, and it is very good indeed.

Preparation time: Serves 4–6
   making and chilling the Moong dal, plus 10 minutes

1 medium-sized onion, peeled and chopped
1 green chilli, seeded (optional) and chopped
1 small bunch of parsley or watercress, stems removed
juice of 1 lemon
400–550g/1–1¼lb leftover cold Moong dal (page 195)

Mix the onion, chopped chilli, parsley or watercress leaves and lemon juice together.

Stir the mixture into the dal and serve cold.

Watercress, celeriac and chicory salad

Hare patton ka salaad

Preparation time: about 10 minutes   *Serves 4–6*

3 bunches of watercress, stems removed
1 small celeriac, peeled and cut in thin juliene strips
2 heads of chicory, divided into leaves
For the dressing
1 tablespoon chopped parsley
1 tablespoon finely chopped onion
1 tablespoon finely chopped cornichons
1 tablespoon chopped capers
½ teaspoon finely chopped garlic
½ teaspoon Dijon mustard
1 teaspoon lemon juice
1½ teaspoons red wine vinegar
2 tablespoons olive oil
salt and freshly ground black pepper

Prepare the vegetables and combine them in a salad bowl.

Mix together the parsley, onion, cornichons, capers and garlic with the mustard, lemon juice and vinegar. Add the oil, season to taste and mix well.

Pour the dressing over the vegetables, and toss well just before serving.

Tomato and onion salad

Tamatar aur piyaz ka salaad

Preparation time: 5 minutes   *Serves 4–6*

3 large tomatoes, cut into wedges
1 medium-sized onion, peeled and very thinly sliced
1 tablespoon chopped fresh basil (optional)
1 tablespoon wine vinegar
1 tablespoon vegetable oil
½ teaspoon freshly ground black pepper
salt

Mix the tomatoes and onion slices in a salad bowl.

Combine the rest of the ingredients and toss them with the tomato and onion mixture.

* The tomato and onion mixture is also delicious with a mixture of plain yoghurt, salt and pepper.

Mushrooms with walnut dressing

Kumbhi akhroot ka salaad

Preparation time: 10 minutes   *Serves 4*

2 tablespoons Dijon mustard
1 tablespoon tarragon vinegar
2 tablespoons walnut oil
225g/8oz button mushrooms, wiped clean
2 tablespoons chopped fresh parsley

Combine the mustard, vinegar and walnut oil.

Slice the mushrooms thinly, pour the mustard mixture over them and toss well.

Sprinkle the parsley over the top and serve.

Tuna salad I

Tuna machli ka pahela salaad

Preparation time: 10 minutes   *Serves 4*

400 g/14 oz canned tuna, drained well and flaked
2 tablespoons mayonnaise
1 tablespoon Dijon mustard
2 spring onions, chopped, or ½ small onion, chopped
4–5 medium-sized mushrooms, sliced
¼ teaspoon freshly ground black pepper
1 fresh green chilli, seeded (optional) and chopped
rye or pumpernickel bread slices, to serve

Combine the tuna, mayonnaise, mustard, spring onions or onion, mushrooms, pepper and chilli.

Serve on open slices of rye or pumpernickel bread.

Tuna salad II
Tuna machli ka doosra salaad

Preparation time: 10 minutes   *Serves 4*

400 g/14 oz canned tuna, drained well and flaked
1 tablespoon chopped fresh parsley
¼ teaspoon cayenne pepper
2 tablespoons mayonnaise
1 tablespoon Dijon mustard
1 medium-sized onion, peeled and chopped
rye or pumpernickel bread slices, to serve

Combine the tuna, parsley, cayenne pepper, mayonnaise, mustard and onion.

Serve on open slices of rye or pumpernickel bread.

Tuna divina

Tuna machli ka teesra salaad

This is what one has for lunch while arguing over what to have for dinner.

Preparation time: 10 minutes   *Serves 4*

400g/14oz canned tuna, drained well and flaked
1 green or red pepper, chopped
12 capers
1 teaspoon coarsely chopped dried red chillies, seeded (optional)
2 teaspoons chopped fresh parsley
juice of 1½ lemons
2 tablespoons Dijon mustard
2 tablespoons olive oil
2 hard-boiled eggs, shelled and chopped
1 medium-sized onion, peeled and chopped
2 tablespoons mayonnaise
rye, pumpernickel or other good bread, to serve

Combine the tuna, pepper, capers, chopped dried chillies, parsley, lemon juice, mustard, oil, eggs, onion and mayonnaise.

Serve on open slices of rye, pumpernickel or other interesting bread.

Pistachio raita
Piston-walla raita

This is more an accompaniment to spicy Indian dishes than a salad, but it is a good one as it cools the palate.

Preparation time: 5 minutes, plus chilling   *Serves 6*

700ml/1¼pt plain yoghurt
4 tablespoons rose water
2 tablespoons clear honey
3 dozen shelled chopped unsalted pistachios
pinch of ground saffron (optional)

Stir the yoghurt, rose water, honey and pistachios together and chill the mixture.

Sprinkle the saffron over the mixture, if wished, and serve.

Beetroot vinaigrette
Seerke-walli saljam

Preparation time: 5 minutes   *Serves 4*

2 tablespoons oil
2 tablespoons tarragon vinegar
pinch of salt
pinch of cayenne pepper
1 tablespoon fresh chopped parsley
6 medium-sized beetroot, boiled, peeled and sliced

Stir together the oil, vinegar, salt, cayenne pepper and parsley. Pour the mixture over the beetroot and serve.

Tarragon-walnut potato salad

Sukhi pati akhroot aur aloo ka salaad

Preparation and cooking time: 15–20 minutes   *Serves 4–6*

2.3 kg/5 lb small, preferably red potatoes
225 ml/8 fl oz mayonnaise
50 ml/2 fl oz walnut oil
2 tablespoons tarragon vinegar
125 ml/4 fl oz Dijon mustard
4 or more large sprigs of fresh dill, chopped
½ teaspoon salt
¼ teaspoon cayenne pepper
2 medium-sized onions, peeled and chopped.

Boil the potatoes in their skins until they are just tender.

Meanwhile, mix together the rest of the ingredients and reserve.

Refresh the potatoes under cold running water for 2–3 minutes only, drain well and cut them in half lengthways.

Mix the mayonnaise mixture into the potatoes, and refrigerate, covered, until ready to serve.

Caraway-onion potato salad

Shazeera-walla piyaz aur aloo ka salaad

Preparation and cooking time: 15–20 minutes   *Serves 4–6*

2.3 kg/5 lb small potatoes
1 large onion, peeled and diced
4 garlic cloves (preferably fresh)
4 tablespoons caraway seeds
4 tablespoons chopped fresh parsley
juice of 2 lemons
4 tablespoons Dijon mustard
4 tablespoons vegetable oil
5 dried red peppers, seeded (optional) and coarsely chopped
½ teaspoon salt

Boil the potatoes in their skins until they are just tender.

Meanwhile, mix together the rest of the ingredients and reserve.

Refresh the potatoes under cold running water for 2–3 minutes only, drain well and cut them in halves lengthways.

Stir the onion mixture with the potatoes, and refrigerate, covered, until ready to serve.

Chicory-walnut salad

Safaid patte akhroot ka salaad

Preparation time: 5 minutes   *Serves 2*

3–4 heads of chicory
2 tablespoons walnut oil
2 tablespoons tarragon vinegar
pinch of salt
handful of chopped walnuts

Cut the heads of chicory across into bite-sized slices and put them in a salad bowl.

Mix the rest of the ingredients together, toss them into the chicory and serve.

* 1–2 garlic cloves, peeled and pressed, are an excellent addition to the dressing as the flavour of garlic is delicious with walnuts.

Chilli-tomato salad

Mirch aur tamatar ka salaad

Preparation time: 5 minutes, plus chilling   *Serves 2*

12 cherry tomatoes or 6 small tomatoes
½ bunch of parsley, stems removed and chopped
½ hot green chilli, seeded (optional) and chopped
1 teaspoon Dijon mustard
1½ teaspoons vegetable oil
2 tablespoons lemon juice
pinch of salt
pinch of cayenne pepper

Halve the cherry tomatoes or quarter the small tomatoes.

Mix the chopped parsley and chilli with the tomatoes, and chill.

Combine the mustard, vegetable oil, lemon juice, salt and cayenne pepper for the dressing and reserve.

Add the dressing to the chilled tomatoes just before serving.

Dressed green salad

Hara salaad

Preparation time: 10 minutes   *Serves 2–4*

1–2 heads of salad greens
2 tablespoons olive oil
juice of ½ lemon
¼ teaspoon freshly, coarsely ground black pepper
salt

Wash and pat the salad greens dry with kitchen paper or a tea towel just before making the salad.

Mix together the rest of the ingredients, toss them well into the leaves and serve immediately.

Tomato mint raita

Phoodina raita

Preparation time: 5–10 minutes   *Serves 4*

2 medium-sized onions, cut in half, then thinly sliced
2 medium-sized tomatoes, peeled and thinly sliced
225 ml/8 fl oz plain yoghurt
3–4 × 25 m/1 in fresh mint sprigs, leaves removed and chopped
5 cm/2 in green chilli, seeded (optional) and finely chopped
¾ teaspoon ground cumin (or ½ teaspoon of chilli powder, if you prefer
   it a bit spicier)
¼ teaspoon salt

Combine the onions and tomatoes with the yoghurt.

Add the mint, chilli, cumin or chilli powder and salt. Mix well
and serve.

Raw spinach salad

Palak salaad

Preparation time: 5–10 minutes   *Serves 4*

3 tablespoons olive oil
2 tablespoons tarragon vinegar
2 tablespoons capers, chopped
1½ teaspoons salt
450g/1 lb spinach, freshly washed, stems removed and dried
1 large onion, preferably red, peeled and thinly sliced

Make the dressing by combining the oil, vinegar, capers and salt.
Just before serving pour the dressing over the spinach and sliced
onion. Toss thoroughly and serve.

* Another very good dressing for this simple salad is made by
combining 2 tablespoons of prepared spicy mustard, juice of 1 large
lemon, and 3 tablespoons of olive oil.

Rice

I never minded inviting friends over to taste my experimental dinners when cooking. Even though I am now more certain of my repertoire, I still enjoy experimenting and still like to whip up something that just 'happens', depending on my mood, my ingredients, and the time I have to cook a meal. After running around all day on appointments, I sometimes have fifteen minutes to cook a meal. Often guests will be arriving soon and I must come up with a meal. But whether you have half a day or fifteen minutes to cook, meals should be prepared with gusto and feeling. This is one of the true enjoyments of cooking, and no doubt I really begin to relax for the first time at the end of the day in my kitchen.

Cooking rice causes great anxiety with some people. This is really unnecessary if, first of all, you tell yourself to *stop worrying*. Do *observe* what you do as you prepare a rice dish. Notice the appearance of the ingredients as you add them — don't just toss in the required amounts. Remember what you are doing. As you gain experience, you will learn to judge the correct proportions by sight. Then you will be able to judge for yourself whether you have added the right amounts, and using scales and a measuring cup will become less and less critical.

In my recipes I have given specific amounts of water for the rice used. To be honest with you, my rule of thumb when cooking rice is to fill the pan with 12mm/½in water above the level of the prepared rice.

If you make a mistake, my feeling is not to bother with great apologies to your guests. This embarrasses most people. Accept the mistake with good grace and learn from it.

There are different kinds of rice available, but before you buy them in bulk, buy smaller quantities of various sorts and try them all until you find the ones you like best. But never, never buy 'instant' rice. It is absolutely dreadful. I do use standard packaged long-grain rice, which is available in every supermarket, but I prefer basmati rice, found in almost all Indian food shops.

Basmati is a special long-grain rice from India and Pakistan that has a unique flavour and aroma. It must be picked over as it sometimes contains small stones and twigs, and washed in several changes of water. This rinses off the excess starch which causes grains of rice to stick together. Basmati rice is then always soaked in more fresh water for thirty minutes or so and drained, but this cuts down on the amount of water used in cooking. The result is worth every instant of extra bother.

Cardamom and coriander rice

Kotmir illaichi-wale chaaval

Preparation and cooking time: about 45 minutes   Serves 6–8

2 tablespoons butter
475g/17oz long-grain rice
4 black cardamom pods
½ teaspoon cayenne pepper
½ teaspoon salt
3 tablespoons finely chopped fresh coriander leaves or parsley

Melt the butter in a saucepan over medium-low heat. Add the rice, cardamom pods and cayenne pepper, and cook for 6–7 minutes, stirring constantly. Watch carefully so the rice does not stick or burn.

Stir in 725 ml/26 fl oz water and the salt. Bring the water to the boil, then cover the pan tightly and cook over very low heat for about 20 minutes, or until the grains are just tender.

Remove the pan from the heat and let the rice rest, covered, for 5–10 minutes.

Sprinkle the chopped coriander or parsley over the rice and serve.

Green pea pillau

Mattar pullao

Preparation and cooking time: about 45 minutes   *Serves 8–10*

225 ml/8 fl oz vegetable oil
3 medium-sized onions, peeled and chopped
2 cinnamon sticks, broken up
25 mm/1 in fresh ginger root, chopped
1 teaspoon chilli powder
¼ teaspoon turmeric
1 teaspoon cumin seeds
575 ml/1 pt water
800 g/28 oz long-grain rice
450 g/1 lb shelled peas, defrosted if frozen
50 g/2 oz butter

Heat the oil in a large saucepan over medium-low heat. When hot, add 2 of the chopped onions, cinnamon sticks, ginger, chilli powder, turmeric and cumin seeds and cook for 10 minutes.

Carefully add the water and bring to the boil. Add the rice, lower the heat and simmer for 15 minutes or until the rice is fluffy.

Add the peas, stir well and cook for a further 10 minutes.

Meanwhile, melt the butter in a pan over medium heat, add the remaining chopped onion, and cook, stirring frequently, until the onion browns and crisps.

Spread the hot onion and butter over the top of the pillau to serve.

Kichri rice

Kichri chaaval

Preparation and cooking time: about 1 hour   *Serves 6*

25 g/1 oz butter
1 medium-sized onion, peeled and chopped
12 cloves
1 cinnamon stick, broken up
¼ teaspoon ground cumin
5 black cardamom pods
¼ teaspoon ground turmeric
150 g/5 oz toor dal, picked over, washed and drained well
400 g/14 oz long-grain rice
2 garlic cloves, peeled and chopped

Melt the butter in a large saucepan over medium-low heat. Add the onion and cook, stirring occasionally, until it begins to brown.

Stir in the cloves, cinnamon, cumin, cardamom and turmeric and cook for 1–2 minutes.

Add the drained dal and continue to cook for another 3–4 minutes, stirring occasionally.

Add 575 ml/1 pt water and bring it to a boil.

Add the rice and garlic, cover tightly, reduce the heat and simmer gently for 40–45 minutes.

Mince pillau

Qeema pullao

Preparation and cooking time: about 45 minutes   *Serves 8–10*

125 ml/4 fl oz vegetable oil
2 medium-sized onions, peeled and chopped
2 cinnamon sticks, broken up
25 mm/1 in fresh ginger root, chopped
1 teaspoon chilli powder
¼ teaspoon turmeric
450 g/1 lb minced beef or lamb
800 g/28 oz long-grain rice
50 ml/2 fl oz plain yoghurt
4 hard-boiled eggs

Heat the oil in a large saucepan over medium-low heat. When hot, add the onions, cinnamon, ginger, chilli powder and turmeric, and cook until the onion browns, stirring occasionally.

Add the meat to the pan and cook, stirring frequently, for 10 minutes.

Add 575 ml/1 pt water to the pan and bring to a boil. Stir the rice in well, add the yoghurt, turn the heat to low and cook, stirring occasionally, for 15 minutes or until the rice is tender.

Shell and quarter the eggs and place them around the pillau to serve.

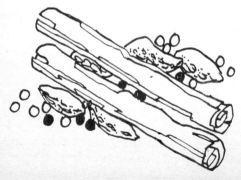

Saffron pillau

Zafrani pullao

I invited Vanessa Redgrave to dinner and hoped that she would
agree to play Olive Chancellor in *The Bostonians*. She loved the
Saffron pillau, the Green lentil dal (page 191), the Baked stuffed
carp (page 60) and the Tomato mint raita (page 175), but said
'no' to *The Bostonians*. The delights of this menu were slow to
act, but effective in the end. Two years later she said 'yes'.

Preparation and cooking time: about 35 minutes   *Serves 3–4*

25 g/1 oz butter
1 cinnamon stick
275 ml/10 fl oz chicken stock
½ teaspoon salt
4 bay leaves, crumbled
450 g/1 lb rice
8 strands of saffron
150 g/5 oz slivered almonds

Melt the butter in a large saucepan with the cinnamon stick.
Add 425 ml/15 fl oz water, the stock, salt and bay leaves, and
bring the liquid to a boil.

Add the rice, cover and cook over very low heat for 10 minutes.

Add the saffron, and cook for another 10 minutes or until the
rice is tender, stirring occasionally.

Sprinkle with the almonds and serve.

Savoury onion rice

Bhuni piyaz ke chaaval

Preparation and cooking time: about 40 minutes   *Serves 8*

25 g/1 oz butter
1 medium-sized onion, peeled and chopped
4 black cardamom pods
425 ml/15 fl oz chicken stock
450 g/1 lb long-grain rice

Melt the butter in a large saucepan over medium-low heat, add the onion, and cook, stirring occasionally, until the onion begins to brown.

Stir in the cardamom pods, then add the stock and 275 ml/ 10 fl oz water. Bring the liquid to a boil.

Add the rice, cover tightly and turn the heat to very low. Cook for 20 minutes or until the rice is tender, stirring occasionally.

Basmati pillau

Basmati pullao

Preparation and cooking time: Serves 4
   1 hour soaking and draining, plus 40 minutes

225 g/8 oz basmati rice, picked over
2 tablespoons vegetable oil
1 medium-sized onion, peeled and chopped
5 cm/2 in cinnamon stick
2 cloves
1 bay leaf, crumbled
125 g/4 oz cashew nuts
50 g/2 oz sultanas
1 level teaspoon salt

Wash the rice in several changes of cold water until the water is clear, then cover it with plenty more cold water and leave it to soak for 30 minutes.

Leave the rice to drain through a sieve for about 30 minutes.

Heat the vegetable oil in a large frying pan over medium-low heat and lightly cook the onion until it is soft.

Add the drained rice, cinnamon, cloves, bay leaf, cashew nuts and sultanas, and stir-fry the mixture for 2 minutes over a medium heat.

Add 575 ml/1 pt water to the pan with the salt. Cover tightly, turn the heat to low and simmer for 20 minutes, adding a little extra water during cooking if necessary, until the rice is tender and fluffy and all the water is absorbed.

Yellow turmeric rice

Peela chaaval

Preparation and cooking time: about 45 minutes   *Serves 8*

25 g/1 oz butter
1 medium-sized onion, peeled and chopped
4 black cardamom pods
425 g/15 fl oz chicken stock
2 teaspoons cumin seeds
¼ teaspoon turmeric
450 g/1 lb long-grain rice

Melt the butter in a large saucepan over medium-low heat. Add the onion and cook, stirring occasionally, until the onion begins to brown.

Add the cardamom, and cook for 1–2 minutes, stirring occasionally.

Add the stock and 500 ml/18 fl oz water. Bring to a boil, then add the cumin seeds, turmeric and rice.

Cook over low heat for 20 minutes or until the rice is tender, stirring occasionally.

Brown rice with bay leaves

Tej pati chaaval

Brown rice is natural rice before it has been stripped of its outer layers, which are high in nutrients.

Preparation and cooking time: about 1 hour   *Serves 4–6*

50g/2oz butter
3–4 bay leaves, crumbled
1 teaspoon salt
400g/14oz brown rice

Melt the butter in a large saucepan over low heat with the bay leaves.

Add 700ml/1¼pt water and the salt to the pan and bring the liquid to the boil.

Add the rice, cover tightly and turn the heat to low. Cook for 45 minutes or until the rice is just tender.

Cashew rice

Kaju chaaval

Preparation and cooking time: about 40 minutes   *Serves 4–6*

425ml/15floz chicken stock
2 dried red chillies, seeded (optional)
1 cinnamon stick, broken up
¼ teaspoon salt
1 teaspoon butter
500g/18oz long-grain rice
150g/5oz shelled raw cashews

Add the stock and 275ml/10floz water to a large saucepan with the chillies, cinnamon stick, salt and butter. Bring the liquid to a boil.

Stir in the rice and cashews, cover tightly and cook over medium heat for 25 minutes or until the rice is tender.

Pulses

Food helps us establish or cement relationships with other people, and this is the aspect of cooking I find most enjoyable. You can do without many things in life but not food and the enjoyment of eating — unless, of course, you become an ascetic or a fakir and become radically self-sufficient. I could never become a hermit, because of missing the deep feeling of accomplishment and communion I have when preparing a meal for friends.

The recipes in this section are made with pulses (dried lentils, beans and peas), which nearly every culture uses in its cooking and which appear at nearly every Indian meal. There are many different varieties, and it is fun discovering the different sorts available from Indian shops. They all have their own particular qualities which you will learn about as you experiment with them. However, there are some general guidelines.

All pulses should be picked over carefully to remove any small stones, papery husks and stems, then washed and drained. Except for the familiar whole green European lentils, most of the whole pulses need overnight soaking covered by about three times their volume of cold water. Because whole Indian pulses are generally smaller than the ones used in the West, most of them need only two hours soaking before they are ready to cook. If they have been hulled and/or split as with *masoor dal*, you can dispense with presoaking altogether. The exception, and naturally there is one, is with *kabli* and *kala chana*. Like their Western counterparts, these chick peas need up to twelve hours presoaking.

This being said, to avoid indigestion be sure to cook the prepared pulses in fresh water until they are tender. Undercooked pulses are bad news.

Some of the most common kinds of pulses used in Indian cooking are as follows:

Chana dal (or *gram dal*) are hulled and split chick peas. Deep yellow in colour, these pulses do not need soaking before cooking.

Kabli chana are yellow chick peas. Unhulled and beige in colour, they need overnight soaking before cooking.

Kala chana are small brown or black chick peas. Like *kabli chana* they require long presoaking and cooking to become tender.

Continental *masoor* are whole greenish-brown lentils. Flat and oval-shaped, they originated in the West and were adopted by India, so they should already be fairly familiar to you. They do not need presoaking.

Masoor are brown Indian lentils. Whole but smaller than continental *masoor*, they do not require presoaking.

Masoor dal are split *masoor* which are tiny and salmon-pink because they have also been hulled. They do not need presoaking and turn yellow when they cook.

Moong beans (or *hari dal*) are dark green, small and round but slightly cylindrical in shape. They need 2–4 hours soaking before cooking, but if oversoaked they will sprout and become moong bean sprouts so familiar in the West.

Moong dal chilka are split *moong* beans, green on one side and pale on the other. They do not need presoaking.

Moong dal are split, light yellow and rectangular in shape because they are hulled. They do not need to be soaked before cooking.

Toor dal (or *arhar dal*) are a hulled, split pulse, a little larger than *chana dal.* Dull and yellow-coloured, they do need presoaking.

Urid (or black *matpe*) are small, dull and black, similar in size and shape to *moong* beans. They must be presoaked.

Urid dal are split *urid* which do not need to be soaked before cooking.

Washed *urid dal* are off-white because they have been hulled and washed as well as split. They do not require presoaking.

This list may seem long and overwhelming, but I suggest that you begin your experience in *dal* cooking with only one or two types of pulses first. Stick to the same type until you are familiar and quite confident with it. Then add another to your repertoire and so on. I would suggest you start with continental *masoor*, which is the most common kind, or possibly *chana dal* or *masoor dal.*

Green lentil dal

Hara masoor ki dal

Preparation and cooking time: *Serves 4–6*
   overnight soaking, plus about 1½ hours

2 tablespoons vegetable oil
1 medium-sized onion, peeled and chopped
12 cloves
½ cinnamon stick, broken
450g/1 lb continental masoor, picked over
400ml/14 floz canned beef consommé
1½ teaspoons salt
1½ medium-sized lemons
½ teaspoon chilli powder

Heat the oil in a saucepan over medium-low heat. When hot, add the onion, and cook, stirring occasionally, until it begins to brown. Stir in the cloves and broken cinnamon stick, and cook for 1 minute.

Add the *masoor* and let cook for 5 minutes, stirring occasionally.

Add the consommé, 850ml/1½pt hot water and the salt. Stir the mixture well, cover and let it cook for 15 minutes.

After 15 more minutes over a medium heat (it will be boiling), add the lemon juice, then toss in the rinds and add the chilli powder. Cook, covered, for another 50 minutes or until the lentils are tender.

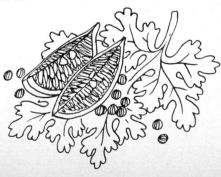

Lemon lentils

Nimbu masoor dal

One of my favourite recipes, this one appeared in the *New York Times Magazine*, March 7 1979. It's also a favourite of many people I've cooked for and has become a staple of my repertoire. I don't recall how it first happened. Probably by finding in the refrigerator a lemon that I flung into a pot of cooking dal in a pretty carefree way, but I always associate it with the actress Felicity Kendal, for whom I first made it.

I regard Felicity as my first pupil. She had come to England right after *Shakespeare-Wallah*, in which she starred, to make a life for herself, rather as the young girl, Lizzie, did in that film. She found a flat in Swan Court, Chelsea, with a tiny kitchen, and I gave her her first lesson in Indian cooking. Our menu was simple: tandoori chicken, pea pillau, raita and lemon dal. Felicity helped me peel onions and to cut up ginger and tried not to get in my way too much. She watched very carefully as she must have watched her English relatives and friends, because in a very short time she was turning out delicious and quite complicated meals in that tiny kitchen, both Indian-style and traditional English ones. She is a natural-born cook, just as she is a natural-born actress; perhaps it is because one needs a sense of innate timing to be successful in both endeavours, cooking and acting.

Preparation and cooking time: Serves 10–12
 overnight soaking, plus about 1½ hours

275 ml/10 fl oz vegetable oil
2 medium-sized onions, halved and thinly sliced
4 × 5 cm/2 in pieces of cinnamon stick
900 g/2 lb masoor dal, picked over and washed
1 tablespoon chopped fresh ginger root
1.1 L/2 pt chicken stock
salt
1 teaspoon cayenne pepper

juice of one lemon, plus the squeezed, seeded skin and pulp
1 small onion, peeled and chopped
1 garlic clove, peeled and finely chopped
1 hot green chilli, chopped, with seeds
4 bay leaves, crumbled
25 g/1 oz chopped fresh coriander leaves

Heat 175 ml/6 fl oz of the oil in a large, deep saucepan over medium-low heat. When hot, add the halved, sliced onions, and cook, stirring, until they soften.

Add the cinnamon, lentils and ginger to the pan, and cook, stirring often, about 10 minutes.

Add the stock and 1.1 L/2 pt hot water, salt to taste and cayenne pepper. Bring to the boil, then simmer about 10 minutes.

Add the lemon juice and squeezed shell, and cook about 50 minutes longer, stirring often.

Heat the remaining oil in a small pan and add the chopped onion, garlic, chilli and bay leaves. Cook, stirring, until the onion is browned.

Add this mixture, including the oil, to the lentils. Sprinkle with the chopped coriander leaves and serve hot.

Chick pea dal

Kabuli chana

Preparation and cooking time: *Serves 6–8*
soaking the pulses, plus 1¼–2¼ hours

6 cups kala chana or brown chick peas, picked over
225 ml/8 fl oz vegetable oil
1 teaspoon chilli powder
¼ teaspoon turmeric
1 teaspoon caraway seeds
1 teaspoon salt
6 garlic cloves, peeled and chopped
1 tablespoon tamarind paste (see below)
4 green chillies, seeded (optional)
1 tablespoon chopped parsley

Soak the *kala chana* overnight in plenty of cold water. If using chick peas, soak for 12 hours. Drain the pulses well.

Heat the oil in a saucepan over medium heat. When hot, add the chilli powder, turmeric and caraway seeds, and cook 2–3 minutes.

Add the drained pulses, stir, and cook for 3–5 minutes more, stirring occasionally.

Add the salt, garlic and the tamarind paste mixed in 125 ml/ 4 fl oz water. Then add 275 ml/10 fl oz hot water and the chillies. Cover tightly and cook over low heat for 2–3 hours or until the pulses are tender, adding more water if necessary. Sprinkle with parsley before serving.

* Tamarind paste is the dark brown pulp of tamarind fruit which has been dried, then soaked and sieved. It has a sour fruity taste and is sold in many Indian food shops.

Green dal with tomato

Moong dal

Preparation and cooking time: *Serves 8–10*
   2 hours soaking, plus about 2¼ hours

700g/1½lb hari dal, picked over
4 tablespoons vegetable oil
1 medium-sized onion, peeled and chopped
1 teaspoon cumin seeds
2 bay leaves, crumbled
12 cherry tomatoes, or 6 small tomatoes
425 ml/15 fl oz chicken stock
1 teaspoon salt
2 dried red chillies, seeded (optional) and chopped

Soak the beans in plenty of water for 2 hours. Drain them well.

Heat the oil in a saucepan over medium-low heat. When hot, add the onion, cumin and bay leaves, and cook, stirring occasionally, until the onion begins to brown.

Add the drained lentils, tomatoes, stock, salt, chillies and 225 ml/8 fl oz hot water. Bring the mixture to a boil, then simmer the mixture over low heat for 2 hours or until the pulses are tender, adding more water as necessary.

Oxtail dal

Gayki dum ki dal

This is a delicious, spicy-hot recipe I really like.

Preparation and cooking time: about 3 hours　　　　*Serves 6–8*

4–6 tablespoons vegetable oil
2 medium-sized onions, peeled and chopped
6 bay leaves, crumbled
12 peppercorns
2 cinnamon sticks, broken up
900g/2lb oxtail, cut in sections
25mm/1in fresh ginger root, chopped
1 green chilli, seeded (optional) and chopped
1 teaspoon chilli powder
450g/1lb masoor dal, picked over, washed and drained

Heat the oil in a large saucepan over medium-low heat. When hot, add the onions, bay leaves, peppercorns and cinnamon sticks, and cook for 5 minutes.

Turn the heat to medium-high, add the oxtail sections, and cook, stirring constantly, until they lose their raw colour on all sides.

Add 1.4L/2½pt water, the ginger, chilli and chilli powder, bring to the boil, then cook over medium-low heat for 2 hours.

Add the drained pulses and 225ml/8floz hot water. Cook over medium heat for 40 minutes, or until the pulses and meat are tender. Serve with plain boiled rice.

Whole green lentils with meat
Masoor ka datcha

Some dal dishes are better very 'wet', but I like this one on the dry side.

Preparation and cooking time: about 1½ hours   *Serves 6–8*

225 ml/8 fl oz vegetable oil
1 large onion, peeled and chopped
2 cinnamon sticks, broken up
1 tablespoon caraway seeds
575 g/1¼ lb continental masoor, picked over, washed and drained well
4 fresh green chillies, seeded (optional)
8 cherry tomatoes or 4 small tomatoes
12 mm/½ in fresh ginger root, chopped
450 g/1 lb lean beef or lamb with some bone, cut in small pieces

Heat the oil in a large saucepan over medium-low heat. When hot, add the onion, cinnamon and caraway seeds, and cook, stirring occasionally, until the onion begins to brown.

Add the lentils and let them cook 7–10 minutes, stirring occasionally.

Add the chillies, tomatoes and ginger, and cook for 7 more minutes, stirring occasionally.

Add 1.4–1.7 L/2½–3 pt hot water, then the meat and bone.

Cook over low heat for another 45 minutes, stirring occasionally. The lentils should be tender and moist, not wet but not too dry. Serve with plain boiled rice and Cucumber raita (page 139).

Spicy chick peas

Channa masaledar

If you are short of time, try this recipe using canned, drained chick peas and about 275 ml/10 fl oz water.

Preparation and cooking time: Serves 4–6
  soaking the dried chick peas, plus 3½–4½ hours

800 g/1¾ lb kabli chana, picked over
6 tablespoons vegetable oil
4–6 bay leaves, crumbled
1 tablespoon cumin seeds
425 ml/15 fl oz canned tomatoes
2 green chillies, seeded (optional)
2 teaspoons salt
2 garlic cloves, peeled and finely sliced
50 g/2 oz chopped fresh parsley

Soak the chick peas in plenty of cold water for 12 hours. Drain them well.

Heat 4 tablespoons of the oil in a saucepan over medium heat. Add the bay leaves and cumin, and cook, stirring, for 1–2 minutes.

Add the canned tomatoes and their liquid, then add the chick peas, chillies, salt and 850 ml/1½ pt hot water.

Bring the liquid to the boil, reduce the heat, cover and simmer for 3–4 hours or until the pulses are tender.

When the chick peas are ready, heat the rest of the oil in a small pan over medium-low heat. When hot, add the garlic and cook until the slices begin to brown, stirring occasionally.

Stir the garlic and the parsley into the chick peas, and cook for a further 10 minutes and serve.

Sweets

Indian sweets are unlike any others in the world. Quantities of milk, nuts, sultanas and sugar are the basic ingredients. The display of sweets is an art in itself, and the *Halwais* (sweetmeat sellers) take great pride in presenting their specialities with care and finesse. The famous *Halwais* had their names stamped on their boxes, like chocolates in the West. Ghaseeta Ram in Bombay is particularly famous for *rasmalai*. In Delhi, Ghante Wala is known for his *sohan halvah*, which is brittle and made in the shape of a heart, with almonds and pistachios decorating it. I cannot give you this recipe as it is jealously guarded as a speciality, so instead I substitute a family version of a famous sweet recipe called *Sheer khorma*.

Decorations of silver and gold foil pounded into feather-light sheets are often stuck on Indian sweets. Saffron is used in them a great deal, but it is now becoming prohibitive to use saffron in great quantities, as it is so expensive. At weddings, receptions and celebrations, great masses of sweets are consumed, and it is considered particularly auspicious to partake generously. Sweets are also the centrepiece of many religious festivals — sweets are brought to the homes of relatives and friends, and they in turn bring them to you.

One of the pleasures of living in a tropical place is the variety of fruits available such as papaya, mango, custard apple, passionfruit, chikoo, ramphal, guava, six to eight different kinds of bananas, loquat, lichee, pineapple, sweet lime — and all this in addition to more common fruits like apples, oranges, tangerines, watermelon, plums, peaches, apricots, cherries etc. Growing up in Bombay, I have known all kinds of fruits and watched foreigners gingerly trying out local fruits for the first time. They often make a face.

There are ten to twelve different kinds of melons in India, but the best ones traditionally come from Afghanistan. Melons from Kabul have almost the consistency of an apple and are a cross in taste between a honeydew and a Cranshaw melon. Of course, we didn't have Cranshaw or honeydew melons in India; they were my introduction to melons in America. I also love the Charentelle melon from France, usually served with a squeeze of lemon or lime, Cointreau and fresh mint. The mint is my added touch to this French dessert, as perfect with the melon as it is in complementing the spiciest Indian dishes.

The displays of fruits closest to the ones I saw in the bazaars of my youth were those I saw in Paris while we were making *Quartet*. I made a sort of 'cornucopia' of fruit salad for the cast and crew, adding mint, red wine, lemon juice and cinnamon to the fruit, and let people top it off with thick *crème fraiche* if they wished. For me, this feast of fruit helped me relive childhood experiences of shopping in the bazaars of Bombay.

Frozen custard apple cream

Sareefe ki rabri

This is not really an ice cream, and if you, unlike me, have more time, you can chill the gelatine and the made pudding in the refrigerator instead of the freezer.

Preparation and cooking time: *Serves 4–6*
  25 minutes, plus 1–2 hours chilling

2 large custard apples
125 g/4 oz cold milk
350 ml/12 fl oz cold double cream
1½ teaspoons powdered gelatine
icing sugar, sifted
few drops of vanilla essence
cracked or cubed ice

Spoon the pulp from the custard apples, discard the seeds and skin and reserve.

Heat half the milk over very low heat, stirring with a wooden spoon. When warmed, immediately pour the milk into a small bowl.

Sprinkle the gelatine into the hot milk and stir it briskly until it is dissolved. Put the mixture in the freezer until it begins to set.

Meanwhile combine the rest of the milk with 225 ml/8 fl oz of the cream in a bowl, and whisk until thick. Add vanilla essence and sift in icing sugar to taste.

Stir the custard apple pulp and thickened milk into the cream and pour the mixture into a serving bowl. Place into the freezer for 1–2 hours.

Whisk the rest of the cream until thick and decorate the pudding with it and serve.

Carrot halva

Gajjar ka halva

Preparation and cooking time: 1 hour   *Serves 6*

pinch of saffron
125 ml/4 fl oz double cream
125 g/4 oz butter, melted
700 g/1½ lb carrots, peeled and grated
50 g/2 oz sugar
4 tablespoons raisins
seeds from 4 black cardamoms
20 blanched almonds, sliced lengthways into slivers
1 tablespoon rosewater
double cream, to serve (optional)

Gently stir the saffron into 2 tablespoons of the cream and gradually mix in the rest of the cream. The cream will take on the colour of the saffron. Do not beat the mixture.

Melt the butter in a heavy saucepan over low heat. Add the grated carrots and stir to coat well.

Stir the sugar, raisins and cardamom seeds into the carrot mixture.

Blend in the saffron and cream mixture, then the almonds. Sprinkle in the rosewater, and cook for 30–40 minutes over a low heat, stirring occasionally. The mixture will become a fairly dry, golden-brown mass.

Serve the halva with double cream poured over the top, if wished.

Spiced fresh pineapple

Masaledar ananas

Preparation time: chilling the pineapple, plus 10 minutes   *Serves 4–6*

1 chilled pineapple
ground cinnamon or freshly grated nutmeg

Peel and slice the pineapple.

Place the slices on a serving dish and shake cinnamon or nutmeg over them.

* A little vanilla essence is another delightful addition to sprinkle over this simple, superb dessert.

Stewed spiced pears

Naaspati ka murabba

Preparation and cooking time: 50 minutes   *Serves 6*

1½ lemons
12 firm, ripe pears, peeled, cored and cut into slices
225 g/8 oz sugar
1 teaspoon vanilla essence
3 cinnamon sticks
½ teaspoon ground cinnamon
75 g/3 oz whole, blanched almonds
double cream, to serve (optional)

Put the lemons in a food processor fitted with the steel blade and process until the lemons are a coarse paste.

Put the lemon paste in a large saucepan with the pears, sugar, vanilla, cinnamon sticks, ground cinnamon and almonds. Cover and cook over medium-low heat for 40 minutes, stirring occasionally.

Remove the cinnamon sticks and serve the stewed pears with double cream, if wished.

Cinnamon-brandy baked pears

Darchini-walli dum naaspati

Preparation and cooking time: about 30 minutes   *Serves 6–8*

9 medium-ripe pears
125 ml/4 fl oz brandy
½ teaspoon vanilla essence
1 teaspoon ground cinnamon
2 tablespoons sugar
double or whipping cream, whipped

Heat the oven to 190C/375F/gas 5. Meanwhile, halve the pears and remove the cores carefully with a spoon or paring knife. Place the pears in a baking dish.

Combine the brandy and vanilla, and pour this over the pears.

Sprinkle the cinnamon and sugar over the mixture, and bake, covered, for 15–20 minutes. The pears should be tender but not too soft.

Serve the pears warm, with whipped cream served separately.

Orange wheels

Santre ke chakle

Preparation and cooking time: 10 minutes, plus chilling   Serves 4–6

6 large oranges, peeled and sliced across in 4–5 rounds each
50 g/2 oz sugar
25 g/1 oz raisins
1 teaspoon ground nutmeg or cinnamon
4 tablespoons rosewater
juice of ½ lemon
2 tablespoons Grand Marnier or other orange liqueur

Peel the oranges, carefully removing all the yellow pith. Slice each one across into 4–5 rounds and put them into a large shallow bowl.

Combine the sugar, raisins, nutmeg or cinnamon, rosewater, lemon juice and Grand Marnier, and pour the mixture over the orange wheels and refrigerate them for at least 2 hours.

Serve the orange wheels, chilled, with some of their juice.

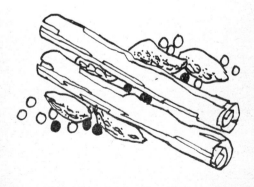

Watermelon ice delight

Tarbooj ki kheer

Preparation and cooking time: 30 minutes, plus freezing   *Serves 4–6*

1 small watermelon
1½ tablespoons gelatine
2 tablespoons milk
150 ml/5 fl oz double cream
few drops of vanilla essence
icing sugar
2 medium-sized egg whites

Halve the melon and scoop out most of the flesh. Remove the seeds and process the flesh into a slush in a food processor or blender.

Soak the gelatine in 125 ml/4 fl oz water and heat the mixture over low heat until the gelatine dissolves.

Cool the gelatine mixture slightly and add it to the watermelon.

Add the milk to the cream and whisk until the cream is thick. Flavour the cream with vanilla essence and a little icing sugar to taste. Stir the cream into the watermelon.

Beat the egg whites until they are stiff but not dry. Fold them well into the melon mixture.

Pour the mixture into a 700 ml/1¼ pt decorative metal mould and freeze for at least 4 hours.

Dip the mould in hot water and turn it out onto a serving plate and serve immediately.

'Quartet' fruit salad

'Quartet' phal ka salaad

This is a dessert served in the film *Quartet*.

Preparation and cooking time: *Serves 8–10*
  15 minutes, plus chilling

425 ml/15 fl oz good red Beaujolais wine
4 teaspoons sugar
2 cinnamon sticks, broken in pieces
juice of 4 lemons
900 g/2 lb ripe strawberries, hulled
4 kiwi fruit, peeled and sliced
2 apples, cored and cubed
450 g/1 lb cherries, seeded
700 g/1½ lb ripe peaches, peeled, seeded and sliced
4 sprigs of fresh mint, stems removed

Pour the wine into a large bowl and add the sugar, cinnamon and lemon juice. Prepare the rest of the ingredients in the order listed, stirring them immediately into the wine mixture.

Chill the mixture in the refrigerator at least 2 hours before serving.

* Though this salad is perfect on its own, you can gild the lily by serving it with *crème fraiche*. Make it by mixing 150 ml/5 fl oz soured cream with 275 ml/10 fl oz double cream and leaving it in a warm room or airing cupboard for 4–5 hours so the cream has a delicious sharpness. Cover and refrigerate it until ready to use.

Pistachio-almond milk pudding

Sheer khorma

On feast days, chicken korma (page 82) was often served, accompanied by a raita made from cucumber, onions and tomatoes mixed in lots of yoghurt. A special bread made in the Muslim areas of Bombay always accompanied these dishes. It was made of layer upon layer of very thin dough topped with nuts. Such a meal would especially be served on Id, the day after the Muslim month of fasting, Ramzan. But the first thing that one ate in the morning after prayers was something sweet. For this special treat, Mother would get up at four in the morning and prepare *sheer khorma*. Fresh milk was brought (it seemed like gallons), and she would cook it slowly and gently in a huge pot.

Meanwhile, we bathed and got ready to go to the mosque for prayers. We were always dressed in completely new clothes, everything new for Id. I remember the crisp smell of these new clothes: kurtas, pyjamas, caps, everything. After prayers we came home to eat the sweet *sheer khorma* and then were taken to visit family and friends where we children would collect gifts of money. After a month of fasting, everyone so enjoyed Id, which is a bit like Easter in Christian countries.

On these visits, we were always offered, on a silver tray, or *thali*, a perfumed essence called *ittar*, the fragrance of which came from the finest natural extracts, rose, mogra, chameli, hina. It was applied, by stopper, to the right hand and ear lobes. Sometimes it spilled onto our clothing and the fragrance seemed to last forever. These rituals meant so much as they bound us together, family and friends.

Preparation and cooking time: *Serves 12*
  overnight soaking, plus about 40 minutes

350g/12oz shelled unsalted pistachios
75g/3oz shelled, unskinned almonds
50g/2oz dried vermicelli
125g/4oz butter
1.1L/2pt milk
175ml/6floz cream
½ teaspoon saffron
5 tablespoons sugar

Place the pistachios and almonds in a bowl and add cold water to cover. Let them stand overnight, then drain and rub off the skins with a tea cloth.

Coarsely grind the nuts in a food processor or blender. Do not over-grind them.

Break the vermicelli in pieces about 10cm/4in long. Melt the butter in a large saucepan and add the vermicelli. Cook, stirring, until the vermicelli is nicely browned without burning.

Add the milk and cream and bring to the boil.

Reduce the heat, add the pistachio mixture, saffron and sugar and simmer, stirring often, about 15 minutes.

Sweet saffron rice with nuts

Meethi taheeri

Preparation and cooking time: Serves 4
  cooking the rice, plus 12–15 minutes

450g/1 lb sugar
¼ teaspoon powdered saffron
40g/1½oz butter
8 cloves
225g/8oz cooked long-grain rice (50g/2oz uncooked rice)
2 tablespoons slivered almonds
2 tablespoons raisins
2 tablespoons sultanas

Simmer the sugar and 125 ml/4 fl oz water until thick and syrupy, 2–3 minutes. Stir in the saffron.

Melt the butter in another saucepan over medium-low heat, add the cloves, and cook until the cloves begin to splutter.

Add the rice and sugar syrup, stir well and add the nuts and dried fruit. Simmer the mixture, covered, for 5 minutes. Serve hot.

Festive sweet yoghurt

Shrikund

Preparation and cooking time: *Serves 4–6*
   2–3 hours draining, plus 10 minutes, then chilling

1 L/1¾pt plain yoghurt
25 g/1 oz shelled almonds
25 g/1 oz shelled, unsalted pistachios
125 g/4 oz icing sugar
½ teaspoon ground cardamom
¼ teaspoon saffron powder
2 tablespoons rosewater

Pour the yoghurt into the middle of a large piece of muslin, gather the corners together and tie them with string or a rubber band and hang the muslin over a bowl for 2–3 hours to drain off the excess water.

Meanwhile, drop the nuts in boiling water and cook for 1 minute. Drain them well and rub off the skins with a tea cloth.

Turn the yoghurt into a clean bowl, add the sugar and mix the two together thoroughly.

Stir in the cardamom, saffron and rosewater, pour the mixture into a glass serving bowl and sprinkle the nuts over the top. Chill well to serve.

Indian rice pudding

Kheer

Preparation and cooking time: 1 hour, plus cooling   *Serves 6–8*

100g/3½oz long-grain rice
1.2L/2¼pt milk
225g/8oz sugar
50g/2oz dried milk
1 tablespoon rosewater
6–8 blanched almonds, chopped
10–12 shelled, unsalted pistachios, chopped
40g/1½oz raisins

Boil the rice in 700ml/1¼pt water until the rice is very soft.

Heat the milk and sugar in another pan and bring them to the boil.

Immediately reduce the heat and stir in the softened rice. Continue cooking over medium-low heat, stirring, until the mixture becomes thick.

Add the dried milk and stir in well.

Add the rosewater, almonds, pistachios and raisins, and remove from the heat.

Let the pudding cool and serve it at room temperature.

Rice, pistachio and almond pudding

Feerni

Preparation and cooking time: *Serves 4–6*
  about 25 minutes, plus chilling

100 g/3½ oz ground rice
1.4 L/2½ pt milk
about 225 g/8 oz sugar
50 g/2 oz dried milk
6–8 shelled, blanched almonds
10 shelled, unsalted pistachios
pinch of ground cardamom

Mix the sugar into the milk, adding more if wished, and heat in a heavy saucepan over medium-high heat.

Stir the ground rice into 225 ml/8 fl oz water.

When the milk begins to boil, remove the pan from the heat and vigorously whisk in the rice liquid to avoid lumps.

When the mixture is smooth, place it over medium-low heat, stir in the dried milk, and cook until thick, whisking occasionally.

Stir in the nuts and cardamom, pour the mixture into small serving bowls and cool. Serve at room temperature or lightly chilled.

Almond sweetmeat

Badam paparh

Preparation and cooking time: *Serves 6–8*
  20–25 minutes, plus 6–8 hours drying

250g/9oz blanched almonds
125g/4oz soft brown sugar

Pound and grind the almonds in a pestle and mortar until they become an oily mass. Alternatively, grind the almonds in a food processor or chop, then grind them in batches in a blender until oily.

Add the sugar and knead the mixture well until it is very smooth and soft.

Divide the almond mixture into 4–6 portions and roll each into a ball. Lightly coat the balls with castor sugar and roll each one out thinly into a round.

Leave the portions to dry on muslin for 6–8 hours.

Store up to 2 weeks separately in greaseproof paper in an airtight container.

Pickles and Chutneys

I first began to cook in earnest in 1958, when I was on my own in New York. Up to then I had dabbled from time to time with cooking, at boy scout outings or school picnics. But in India cooking in the home is not really something family men do. Cooking is either done by a hired cook (often a man) or, more usually, by one's mother and sisters. As a child I spent a certain amount of time in the kitchen, the centre of activity in our large household. I watched and listened and tasted continually. Shopping with my father and hearing the family's many discussions and comments about food, I quite naturally absorbed a great deal without being aware. These things awakened my interest in cooking and made it quite a natural part of life.

It dawned on me that each family has a distinctive way of cooking, passed on from one generation to the next. This is why the same classic Indian dishes never taste exactly the same in different homes you visit. Each one has its own style or 'taste' somehow bequeathed by grandmother to mother to daughters and, occasionally, to a son like myself. If my father were ever to cook, I'm sure he would also make wonderful dishes with the same family 'taste'.

In this chapter I have included some of my family's recipes for pickles. You will also find 'Hamida Begum's Lime Pickle' recipe, which figures so importantly in my film *The Courtesans of Bombay*. It is a very old recipe whose origins are probably ancient and is one of the few recipes in this book which will really take a lot of time to make. But the result is well worth the effort.

In India we never stored pickles and chutneys in the refrigerator, but in a cool, dark area. Because I always have a refrigerator available, I tend to store my pickles and chutneys, well sealed, in it.

Mixed vegetable pickle

Sabji ka aachar

Preparation and cooking time: *Makes about .8 L/1½pt pickle*
  1 hour soaking, plus 30 minutes, then cooling

1 medium-sized cauliflower
125g/4oz green beans, topped and tailed and cut across in half
1 medium-sized carrot
275ml/10floz distilled or white wine vinegar
150ml/5floz vegetable oil
8 bay leaves, crumbled
12 garlic cloves, peeled and roughly chopped
2 tablespoons sugar
6 black peppercorns
salt
For the masala
9 red chillies, seeded (optional) and chopped
½ teaspoon yellow mustard seeds
½ teaspoon ground fenugreek leaves
5cm/2in fresh ginger root, grated
3 green chillies, seeded (optional)
2 teaspoons cumin seeds

Cut the cauliflower into florets and the carrot into slices about
6mm/¼in thick.

Mix and wash the vegetables, then cover them with fresh cold
water for 1 hour.

Drain the vegetables well and leave them in a colander.

Grind the *masala* spices together in a pestle and mortar, adding a
little of the vinegar to make a paste.

Heat the oil in a large frying-pan over medium-low heat. When
hot, add the garlic and bay leaves, and cook, stirring frequently,
for 2–3 minutes.

Add the *masala* paste to the pan and fry for a further 5 minutes.

Add the sugar, vegetables, peppercorns, salt to taste and remaining vinegar to the pan. Cook over low heat until the vegetables soften.

Remove the mixture from the heat and let it cool. Transfer it to a clean glass or ceramic jar and cover with a non-metallic, airtight lid. Store in a cool, dark place.

Broccoli pickle

Broccoli ka aachar

Preparation and cooking time: *Makes about .8 L/1½pt pickle*
   15 minutes, plus 1 week maturing

700g/1½lb broccoli florets with tender stems attached (about 1.5 kg/ 3 lb including tough stalks)
1 bunch of dill, stemmed and chopped
1 tablespoon yellow mustard seeds
5–10 garlic cloves, peeled and chopped
275 ml/10 fl oz vinegar
1 teaspoon salt
1 tablespoon vegetable oil
25 mm/1 in fresh ginger root, coarsely grated

Put all the ingredients and 275 ml/10 fl oz water into a glass jar or jars and top with non-metallic, airtight lids. Shake to mix well.

Allow the pickle to mature in a cool, dark place for 1 week, shaking occasionally.

Parveen's tomato chutney

Parveen ki tamatar chutni

Preparation and cooking time: *Makes about 425 ml/15 fl oz chutney*
   3–3½ hours

1.6 kg/3½ lb tomatoes
425 ml/15 fl oz white wine vinegar
½ teaspoon salt
25 g/1 oz raisins
5 cm/2 in fresh ginger root, finely grated
1 garlic clove, peeled and pressed
1½ teaspoons ground cumin
½ teaspoon cumin seeds
8 cloves
6–8 black peppercorns
1 cinnamon stick, broken in pieces
125 g/4 oz sugar
2 teaspoons chilli powder

Wash the tomatoes, shake them dry and put them in a large saucepan with 350 ml/12 fl oz vinegar and salt. Cover and heat them until the vinegar boils, then reduce the heat and simmer, uncovered, until the tomatoes become just tender, 8–10 minutes.

Remove the tomatoes from the pan with a slotted spoon and set them aside.

Meanwhile, soak the raisins in the remaining vinegar for at least 30 minutes.

Mix the ginger, garlic and ground cumin to a fine paste, mix in the cumin seeds and reserve.

Pound the cloves, peppercorns and cinnamon together in a pestle and mortar.

Put the tomatoes in a dry saucepan, add the sugar and place over medium-low heat. Cook until the sugar melts, stirring occasionally.

Add the garlic paste and the clove mixture to the pan, then stir in the raisins and their soaking liquid and the chilli powder. Cover and cook for 2 hours or until the mixture is thick.

Remove the pan from the heat, add salt if necessary, and allow the chutney to cool completely.

Transfer the chutney to clean glass or ceramic jars and cover with non-metallic, airtight lids. Store in a cool, dark place.

Green chilli and lime pickle

Hari mirch nimboo ka aachar

Preparation and cooking time: *Makes about .8 L/1½pt pickle*
   30 minutes, plus cooling

500g/18oz green chillies
15 limes
3 tablespoons mustard powder
100g/3½oz salt
225ml/8floz vegetable oil
½ teaspoon ground asafoetida
¼ teaspoon ground fenugreek leaves
1 teaspoon turmeric

Wash the chillies, removing any stalks, and dry them well.

Cut the limes in half, extract the juice and discard the flesh.

Mix the lime juice with the mustard powder and salt.

Heat the oil until nearly boiling. Remove it from the heat and add the asafoetida, fenugreek and turmeric.

Stir in the mustard mixture and green chillies, mixing well. When cool, transfer the mixture to clean glass or ceramic jars and cover with non-metallic, airtight lids. Store in a cool, dark place.

Tomato chutney

Tamatar chutni

Preparation and cooking time:
  2¼–2¾ hours, plus cooling

Makes about .8 L/1½pt chutney

2 lemons
2.3 kg/5 lb tomatoes
275 ml/10 fl oz white wine vinegar
350 g/12 oz sugar
2 teaspoons cayenne pepper
150 g/5 oz raisins
1 cinnamon stick, broken into small pieces
150 g/5 oz slivered almonds

Seed and chop the lemons, reserving the juice. Transfer the lemons and juice to a food processor or in batches to a blender and process them to shreds.

Combine the tomatoes, vinegar, sugar, cayenne pepper, raisins, cinnamon, almonds, shredded lemons and 425 ml/15 fl oz water in a deep saucepan. Bring the mixture to a boil.

Reduce the heat and simmer, stirring occasionally until the liquid boils almost all away, 2–2½ hours.

Remove the chutney from the heat and let it cool. Transfer it to a clean glass or ceramic jar or jars and cover with a non-metallic, airtight lid or lids. Store in a cool, dark place.

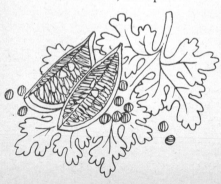

Spicy carrot hors d'oeuvre

Gajjar ka aachar

Preparation time: *Serves 4*
  5–10 minutes, plus chilling

6 medium-sized carrots
4 tablespoons vegetable oil
1–1½ teaspoons chilli powder
1 tablespoon caraway seeds
juice of ½ lemon
½ teaspoon salt
2 teaspoons chopped fresh dill or ½ teaspoon dill weed (optional)

Cut the carrots lengthways into sticks, then halve them once and place them into a bowl.

Whisk the oil, chilli powder, caraway seeds, lemon juice and salt together.

Pour the mixture over the carrot sticks, toss it well in and refrigerate. Serve chilled, sprinkled, if wished, with chopped fresh dill or dill weed. Keeps refrigerated, covered, up to a week.

Mango chutney

Ambia ki chutni

Preparation and cooking time: *Makes about 425 ml/15 floz chutney*
  about 40 minutes, plus overnight maceration and cooling

1 kg/2¼ lb ripe mangoes
425 ml/15 floz vinegar
750 g/26 oz soft dark brown sugar
salt
1½ teaspoons chilli powder
25 mm/1 in fresh ginger root, finely chopped
50 g/2 oz assorted chopped dry fruit and nuts such as sultanas,
  currants, walnuts, dates and cashews

Peel the mangoes finely, then cut the flesh into slices.

Place the raw mangoes in a glass or ceramic bowl or other container and add the vinegar, soft dark brown sugar, salt, chilli powder and chopped ginger. Stir well, cover and leave overnight to macerate.

The next day, transfer the mixture to a stainless steel saucepan and cook over low heat, stirring frequently, until the mixture begins to thicken.

Add the chopped fruit and nuts and continue cooking, stirring frequently to prevent burning, until the mixture is thick.

Remove the pan from the heat. When the chutney is cool enough, correct the seasoning with more salt, chilli powder and vinegar to taste.

Transfer the chutney to a clean dry glass or ceramic jar or jars and seal with non-metallic, airtight lids. Store in a cool, dark place.

Hamida Begum's stuffed lime pickle

Bhare nimboo ka aachar

This recipe, which figures prominently in *The Courtesans of Bombay*, will produce enough pickle to last an entire family for quite a long time, as one can imagine. It is so good that there is always great demand for it from friends and family. You can, of course, reduce the quantities proportionally.

Preparation and cooking time: *Makes about 5.5 L/9¾ pts pickle*
   2½–3 hours, plus cooling and bottling

200 limes
600g/20oz dried red chillies
225g/8oz mustard seeds
125g/4oz cumin seeds
125g/4oz onion seeds
450g/1 lb garlic cloves, peeled
450g/1 lb salt
850ml/1½pt mustard oil
12 green chillies

Squeeze the juice of 100 limes into a large bowl, cover and reserve.

Put the rest of the limes in a large saucepan or preserving pan, cover with plenty of water, bring to a boil and simmer until they are tender.

Drain the limes, dry them with a tea towel and put them aside.

Take the red chillies and pound them finely in a pestle and mortar or grind them in a food processor or in batches in a blender.

Put the mustard seeds in a frying-pan over low heat and dry-roast them for 2–3 minutes, shaking the pan occasionally. The seeds should begin to release their aroma.

Repeat with the cumin seeds and then the onion seeds.

Combine the mustard, cumin and onion seeds. Take two-thirds

of the mixture and pound it finely in a pestle and mortar or grind it in a food processor or in batches in a blender.

Blend the remaining seed mixture with the ground red chillies and the pounded or ground seed mixture.

Pound the garlic cloves into a paste in a pestle and mortar or a food processor or in batches in a blender with a little water, then drain off the water.

Mix the garlic with the chilli and seed mixture, adding the salt and a little of the lime juice to make a paste.

Cut the boiled limes only half-way down into 4. Spread the spice paste well into the limes, put them in a large container and add the rest of the lime juice.

Warm the oil until it begins to sputter, then pour it over the stuffed limes and whole green chillies.

When the mixture is cool enough, transfer it to glass or ceramic bottles and cover with non-metallic, airtight lids. Store in a cool, dark place.

Coconut and mint chutney

Khopra poodina ki chutni

This is delicious with roasted meats and fowl.

Preparation and cooking time: 50 minutes–1 hour   *Serves 6–8*

1 fresh coconut
leaves of 4 mint sprigs
juice of 1 lemon
2 hot green chillies, seeded (optional)

Heat the oven to 200C/400F/gas 6.

Bake the coconut for 15 minutes.

Place the hot coconut on concrete or another hard surface and smash it open with a hammer.

When they are cool enough, peel away the brown papery skin and the white meat with a potato peeler. Chop any large pieces, if necessary, into smaller ones.

Put the coconut and the rest of the ingredients in a food processor or blender, in batches and with a little extra water if necessary, and process the mixture to a paste. Serve the chutney fresh. It can be stored, well covered, in the refrigerator for 1–2 days.

Sweet peach chutney

Meethe shaftaloo ki chutni

This sweet chutney is great when used as a complement to main dishes or to top ice cream as a dessert.

Preparation and cooking time: *Makes about 5 × 750 ml/1¼ pt jars*
*   about 3 hours, plus cooling*

4.5 kg/10 lb firm ripe peaches
2 cinnamon sticks
225 ml/8 fl oz medium-dry sherry
6 cardamom pods
450 g/1 lb sugar
150 g/5 oz raisins
125 ml/4 fl oz lemon juice
1 teaspoon almond essence

Heat a large saucepan of water to the boil and remove from heat. Drop in 8–12 peaches, leave for 1 minute, then remove 1 peach and peel off the skin and set it aside. Repeat with the other peaches in the water.

Continue soaking the rest of the peaches, a few at a time, in the hot water, reheating it if necessary, peeling and setting them aside.

Halve and stone the peaches, then chop the flesh.

Combine the peaches, cinnamon, sherry, cardamom pods, sugar, raisins, lemon juice and almond essence in a large saucepan or preserving pan. Bring the mixture to a boil, stirring frequently.

Reduce the heat and simmer over medium-low heat for 2 hours or until the mixture becomes very thick, stirring frequently. Reduce the heat, if necessary, to prevent burning.

When the chutney is cool enough, transfer it to clean, dry glass or ceramic jars and cover with non-metallic, airtight lids. Store in a cool, dark place.

Ginger pickle

Adrak ka aachar

Preparation and cooking time: *Makes about 425 ml/15 fl oz pickle*
    10 minutes, plus 1 week maturing

8 × 10 cm/4 in fresh root ginger, finely peeled
850 ml/1½ pt distilled or white wine vinegar
275 ml/10 fl oz mustard oil
2 tablespoons yellow mustard seeds
12 garlic cloves, peeled and halved lengthways
½ tablespoon salt
6 green chillies

Put all the ingredients in a large glass jar or jars and top with non-metallic, airtight lids. Shake to mix well.

Allow the pickle to mature for 1 week in a cool, dark place, shaking occasionally.

Cauliflower pickle

Phool gobi ka aachar

Preparation and cooking time: *Makes about 425 ml/15 fl oz pickle*
    10 minutes, plus 1 week maturing

1 medium-sized cauliflower, cut into florets
1 green chilli, seeded (optional) and chopped
5–10 garlic cloves, peeled and coarsely chopped
275 ml/10 fl oz vinegar
2 teaspoons salt
1 teaspoon turmeric
1 teaspoon caraway seeds
5 cm/2 in fresh ginger root, coarsely grated
1 tablespoon vegetable oil

Put all the ingredients and 275 ml/10 fl oz water into a large glass jar or jars and top with non-metallic, airtight lids. Shake to mix well.

Allow the pickle to mature for 1 week in a cool, dark place, shaking occasionally.

Mango relish

Aam chhunda

Preparation and cooking time: *Makes about 425 ml/15 fl oz relish*
    about 40 minutes, plus cooling

1 kg/2¼ lb mangoes
1 kg/2¼ lb sugar
50 g/2 oz salt
5–6 black peppercorns
1½ teaspoons chilli powder
2–3 black cardamom pods, coarsely pounded

Wash, dry, peel and grate the mangoes into a saucepan.

Stir in the sugar and place the pan over low heat, stirring continually with a wooden spoon for about 30 minutes.

When the mixture changes colour and falls into a thread when lifted with the spoon, remove from heat.

Stir in the salt, pepper and chilli powder with the coarsely pounded cardamom pods. Let the mixture cool.

Transfer the mixture to a clean, dry glass jar and cover with a non-metallic, airtight lid. Store in a cool, dark place.

Index

Note: Contributions by the people concerned are indicated by *italic* page references.

Adeane, Edward 18
Almond
  pistachio milk pudding 208–9
  saffron pillau with almonds 183
  spiced lamb with almonds 130
  sweetmeat 214
Asparagus, fresh, in mustard dressing 157
Aubergine
  and beef casserole, North Indian 116
  stewed 156
Autobiography of a Princess 15
Avocado and tomato soup 37

Baked
  lamb with chilli and ginger 105–6
  mackerel and tomatoes 55
  red snapper 56
  sea bass with cumin and tomatoes 63
  spicy beefburgers 121
  stuffed carp 60
  trout in mushroom vinaigrette 59
Basmati pillau 185
Baxter, Anne 32
Beef 115–28, 182, 197
  and aubergine casserole, North Indian 116
  cubed 126
  cubed with spring onions and chillies 118–19
  ginger roast 127
  green lentils with 197
  kebabs, spicy minced 125
  potato cakes, spicy 119–20
  rib roast, Merchant-style 115
  soup, hearty 38
Beefburgers, baked spicy 121
Beer and lemon 30
Beetroot vinaigrette 170
Bergman, Ingrid 15, 16, 20, 21
Bluefish in coconut sauce 50
Boiled potatoes with spring onions and chives 135
Bombay vegetable fritters 26
Bostonians, The 183
Brandy-cinnamon baked pears 204
Broccoli
  and lemon gazpacho 32
  in garlic-lemon butter 155
  pickle 217
Brown, Kay 20, 21
Brown rice with bay leaves 186–7
Buitons, Raimond 18

Cabbage
  red, and raisins, sautéed 154
  red, spicy 153
Callow, Simon *16–17*
Caraway 8
  and ginger, roast lamb with 111
  -cayenne roast chicken 71
  -onion potato salad 172
  -tomato egg curry 97
Cardamom 8
  and coriander rice 179
Carp, baked stuffed 60

Carrot
  halva 202
  cinnamon-dill 152
Cashew
  and lamb stew 128–9
  rice 187
Cauliflower
  and potatoes, spicy stewed 151
  and tomatoes, stewed 150
  pickle 227
  potatoes and peas, spicy 141
Cayenne 8
  -caraway roast chicken 71
  cayenned corn 149
Celeriac, watercress and chicory salad 165
'Chaat', potato 146
Chestnut stuffing for turkey 96
Chick peas 189–90
  dal 194
  spicy 198
Chicken 69–90
  soups made with stock 32–43
  stuffings for 73–6
  breasts, sauce for 87
  breasts sautéed with chilli and cinnamon 79
  caraway-cayenne roast 71
  chilli-ginger roast
  curry, spicy 88–9
  in coconut sauce 84
  korma, 82; accompaniments 82, 208
  livers baked in spicy mustard 90
  livers baked in spicy yoghurt 89
  pepper 86
  Richard's 87
  spicy mustard 83
  tandoori 78
  tomato 85
  yoghurt 80–1
Chicory
  -walnut salad 173
  watercress and celeriac salad 165
Chilli 8, 10
  and cinnamon, chicken breasts sautéed with 79
  and ginger, baked lamb with 105–6
  and lime pickle 219
  and parsley stuffing for chicken 74
  and spring onions, cubed beef with 118–19
  -ginger roast chicken 72
  lemon and ginger stuffing for chicken 73
  paste for lamb 128–9
  -tomato salad 173–4
Chives
  chive and mustard prawn bites 24
  and spring onions, boiled potatoes with 135
Chutney 218–19, 220, 222, 225–6
  fresh 221, 224–5
  storage 69, 215
  and pancakes stuffing for chicken 75

Cinnamon 10
  and chilli, chicken breasts sautéed with 79
  -brandy baked pears 204
  -dill carrots 152
Claverack carrot soup 36
Cloves 10
  clove curried eggs 98
  clove garlic mixed vegetables 148
Coconut
  and mint chutney 224–5
  dumplings and vegetable stew 160–1
  prawns, spicy 53
  sauce, chicken in 84
  sauce, mackerel or bluefish in 50
  sauce, spicy 52
  sauce, spicy, lobster in 51
Cod
  curry, spicy 66
  pillau 61
Cod's roe, spicy 48
Coriander 10
  and cardamom rice 179
Courgettes
  grilled, with cumin butter 159
  sautéed 145
Courtesans of Bombay, The 215, 223
Cream and mustard sauce for chicken breasts 87
Crème fraîche 200, 207
Crown roast of lamb, Merchant-style 114–15
Cubed
  beef 126
  beef with spring onions and chillies 118–19
  lamb with mustard and bay 106–7
Cucumber raita 139
Cumin 11
  and tomatoes, baked sea bass with 63
  butter, grilled courgettes with 159
Curried fish in yoghurt 47
Curry
  fish, spicy 66
  spicy chicken 88–9
  spicy vegetarian 140
  tomato-caraway egg 97
  tomato lamb 109

Dal
  types 190
  recipes 191–8
  chick pea 194
  green lentil 191
  green, with tomato 195
  oxtail 196
Deep-fried Cheddar balls 25
Delhi Way, The 12
Dressed green salad 174
Drinks 28–30
Duck, roast stuffed 91–2

Eggs 97–102
  egg curry, tomato-caraway 97
  egg salad 99
  clove-curried 98
  Ismail's 102
  scrambled, mustard 101
  souffléd scrambled 100–1
Europeans, The 1

'Fasting Day' potatoes 158–9

Festive sweet yoghurt 211
Fish 24, 27, 45–68
  to use leftover 61
  curried, in yoghurt 47
  curry, spicy 66
  pillau 61
  roe, spicy 48
Fox-Pitt, Sarah *17–18*
Fresh
  asparagus in mustard dressing 157
  mushroom soup 42
  sardine snacks 27
  vegetable toast 147
Frozen custard apple cream 201

Garlic 9
  and clove mixed-vegetables 148
  -lemon butter, broccoli in 155
Gazpacho
  broccoli and lemon 32
  Indian 33
  soup, white 43
Giblet
  and kheema stuffing for chicken 76
  stuffing for turkey 95
Gin and tonic 29
Ginger 9
  and caraway, roast lamb with 111
  and chilli, baked lamb with 105–6
  and mustard, roast veal with 132
  beef, roast 127
  broccoli soup 34
  chicken 77
  -chilli roast chicken 72
  lemon and chilli stuffing for chicken 73
  pickle 226
Gingerburgers 122
Green beans in mustard sauce 155–6
Green chilli and lime pickle 219
Green dal with tomato 195
Green lentil
  dal 191
  salad 164
  green lentils, whole, with meat 197
Green pea pillau 180
Green salad, dressed 174
Goose, roast stuffed 92–3
Grilled
  courgettes with cumin butter, 159
  halibut 57

Haddock
  curry, spicy 66
  grilled 57
  pan-braised 58
Halibut, grilled 57
Hamida Begum's stuffed lime pickle 223–4
Hari dal 190, 195
Hearty soup 38
Hot rough tomato soup 35
Husain, Begum Sabeeha Ahmed 1

Indian
  gazpacho 33
  rice pudding 212
Ismail's
  duck stuffing 92
  egg salad 99
  eggs 102
  spicy fish roe 48

superb turkey stuffing 96
Ivory, James 1, *12–13*, 15, 19, 31

Jaffrey, Madhur 4, 18
Jaffrey, Saeed 4, 13
Jane Austen in Manhattan 32
Jhabvala, Ava 20
Jhabvala, Ruth Prawer 1, 15, 20

Kapoor, Sanjana 19
Kapoor, Shashi 84
Kebabs 103
    minced lamb 131
    spicy minced beef 125
Kendal, Felicity *18–20*, 83, 192
Kendal, Jennifer 19, 97
Kichri rice 191
Korner, Anthony *14–16*
Korner, Sandra *20–1*

Lal mirch 8, 10
Lamb 105–15, 124–5, 128–31, 182, 197
    and cashew stew 128–9
    baked, with chilli and ginger 105–6
    chops, North Indian 113
    crown roast of 114–15
    cubed, with mustard and bay 106–7
    curry, tomato 109
    green lentils with 197
    kebab, minced 131
    pan-roasted 107
    roast, with ginger and caraway 111
    spiced Kashmiri 130
    stew, Rajasthani, spicy 108
    stew, spicy 110
    with onions and tomatoes 112
Lemon
    and broccoli gazpacho 32
    -garlic butter, broccoli in 155
    ginger and chilli stuffing for chicken 73
    lentils 192–3
Lentils
    types 190
    lentil dal, green 191
    lentil salad, green 164
    lentil soup, red 40
    lemon 192–3
    whole green, with meat 197
Lime
    and green chilli pickle 219
    pickle, Hamida Begum's stuffed 223–4
Lobster in spicy coconut sauce 51

Mackerel
    and tomatoes, baked 55
    baked 56
    in coconut sauce 50
    curry, spicy 66
    sautéed with mustard and dill 54
Mackey, Nicole 18
Mango
    chutney 222
    relish 228
Masalas 8, 49, 119–20, 140
Masoor 191–3
    types 190
Melons 199–200
Merchant's spinach purée 142
Miller, Allen 24
Miller, Jeannie 24

Mince
    pillau 182
    with peas 123
    with peas Kashmiri-style 124
    with potatoes 123
    with spinach 123
Minced
    lamb kebab 131
    meat with giblet stuffing for chicken 76
Mint
    and coconut chutney 224–5
    raita, tomato 175
Mirch, lal 8, 10
Misra, Caroline 18
Misra, Ravi 18
Mixed vegetable pickle 216–17
Moong dal 190, 195; to use leftover 164
Mullet
    baked 56
    curry, spicy 66
    grey, baked stuffed 60
Mushroom
    soup, fresh 42
    vinaigrette, baked trout in 59
    sautéed 138
    sautéed in mustard oil 138
    with walnut dressing 166–7
Mustard
    and bay, cubed lamb with 106–7
    and chive prawn bites 24
    and cream sauce for chicken breasts 87
    and dill, mackerel sautéed with 54
    and dill, prawns with 65
    and ginger, roast veal with 132
    chicken livers baked in spicy 90
    chicken, spicy 83
    dressing, fresh asparagus in 157
    prawns 62
    sauce, green beans in 155–6
    scrambled eggs 101
    seeds 9

North Indian beef and aubergine casserole
    116
North Indian lamb chops 113

Omelette fines herbes 100
Onion
    and tomato salad 166
    -caraway potato salad 172
Orange wheels 205
Oxtail dal 196

Pancakes and chutney stuffing for chicken 75
Pan-braised haddock 58
Pan-roasted lamb 107–8
Parker, Phyllis 43
Parsley and chilli stuffing for chicken 74
Parveen's tomato chutney 218–19
Pears
    cinnamon-brandy baked 204
    stewed spiced 203–4
Pepper chicken 86
Pickles 216–17, 219, 223–4, 226–8
    storage 69, 215
Pillau
    Basmati 185
    fish 61
    mince 182
    pea 180

prawn 67–8
saffron 183
Pineapple, spiced fresh 203
Pistachio
  -almond milk pudding 208–9
  raita 170
Plaice pillau 61
Pomfret, spicy fried 49
Potato
  cakes, spicy beef 119–20
  'chaat' 146
  patties, stuffed 144–5
  salad, caraway-onion 172
  salad, tarragon-walnut 171
  to use leftover 146
Potatoes
  and cauliflower, spicy stewed 151
  and peas 136
  boiled, with spring onions and chives 135
  cauliflower and peas, spicy 141
  'Fasting Day' 158–9
Prawn pillau 67–8
Prawns
  mustard 62
  spicy coconut 53
  with mustard and dill 65
  yoghurt 64
Puddings 201, 203–13
Pulses
  how to prepare 189
  types 189–90

Quartet 16, 88, 200, 207
'Quartet' fruit salad 207

Raisins and red cabbage, sautéed 154
Raita
  cucumber 139
  pistachio 170
  tomato mint 175
Rajasthani spicy lamb stew 108
Ramsay, Peggy 16
Raw spinach salad 176
Red cabbage
  and raisins, sautéed 154
  spicy 153
Red lentil soup 40
Red snapper, baked 56
Redgrave, Vanessa 183
Reeve, Christopher 78
Rib roast, beef 115
Rice
  how to cook 177–8
  types 19, 177–8
  brown, with bay leaves 186–7
  cardamom and coriander 179
  cashew 187
  kichri 181
  pillau, *see* Pillau
  pistachio and almond pudding 213
  pudding, Indian 212
  savoury onion 184
  sweet saffron, with nuts 210
  yellow turmeric 186
Richard's
  chicken 87
  cinnamon-dill carrots 152
Roast
  ginger beef 127
  lamb with ginger and caraway 111

stuffed duck 91
stuffed goose 92–3
stuffed turkey 94
veal with mustard and ginger 132
Robbins, Richard 1, *13–14*, 19, 163
Rodman, Michael 19
Room With a View, A 1, 17, 88
Rose, Joanna 39
Royal kofta (meatballs) 117–18

Saffron 9, 199
  pillau 183
  rice, sweet, with nuts 210
Salads 99, 163–76
Salmon
  curried in yoghurt 47
  curry, spicy 66
  pillau 61
Salty lassi 28
Sautéed
  courgettes 145
  mushrooms 138
  red cabbage and raisins 154
Savages 14
Savoury onion rice 184
Scrambled mustard eggs 101
Sea bass, baked with cumin and tomatoes 63
Shakespeare-Wallah 192
Sheer khorma 199, 208–9
Smith, Anthony 18
Smith, Maggie 88
Sorrel soup 39
Souffléd scrambled eggs 100–1
Spices 8–11
Spiced
  fresh pineapple 203
  Kashmiri lamb 130
  okra 157–8
Spicy
  beef potato cakes 119–20
  carrot hors d'oeuvre 221
  chick peas 198
  chicken curry 88–9
  coconut prawns 53
  coconut sauce 52
  fish curry 66
  fried pomfret 49
  fruit goose stuffing 93
  minced beef kebabs 125
  mustard chicken 83
  potatoes, cauliflower and peas 141
  red cabbage 153
  stewed cauliflower and potatoes 151
  turkey stuffing 95
  vegetarian curry 140
Spinach
  Jannu 143
  purée 142
  salad, raw 176
  stuffing for potato patties 144–5
Spring onions
  and chillies, cubed beef with 118–19
  and chives, boiled potatoes with 135
Stamp, Terence 18
Stewed
  aubergine 156
  cauliflower and tomatoes 150
  spiced pears 203–4
Stuffed potato patties 144–5
Sweet lassi 28

peach chutney 225–6
saffron rice with nuts 210

Tamarind
    paste 194
    water 140
Tandoori chicken 78
Tarragon-walnut potato salad 171
Tomato
    and avocado soup 37
    and onion salad 166
    -caraway egg curry 97
    chicken 85
    -chilli salad 173–4
    chutney 218–19, 220
    green dal with 195
    lamb curry 109
    mint raita 175
    soup, hot rough 35
    soup with avocado 37
Toor dal 190
'Tortilla' eggs with parsley and chilli 99
Trout, baked, in mushroom vinaigrette 59
Tuna
    divina 169
    salad 167, 168
Turbot
    curried in yoghurt 47
    grilled 57
    pillau 61
Turkey, roast stuffed 94–7

Turmeric 10
    rice, yellow 186

Va-va-voom potatoes 137
Veal, roast, with mustard and ginger 132
Vegetables
    buying 133–4
Vegetarian curry, spicy 140
Vodka with soda or tonic and mint 29

Walnut
    -chicory salad 173
    dressing, mushrooms with 166–7
    -tarragon potato salad 171
Watercress
    and potato soup 41
    celeriac and chicory salad 165
Watermelon ice delight 206
White gazpacho soup 43
Whole green lentils with meat 197

Yellow turmeric rice 186
Yoghurt
    beef dishes with 116–18, 122–4
    chicken dishes with 80–82, 89
    drinks 28
    lamb dishes with 108, 110, 112–13, 128–31
    see also raitas
    festive sweet 211
    fish curried in 47
    prawns 64

Index of Indian Titles

Aam chhunda 228
Adrak aur shazeera-walli ran 111
Adrak broccoli walla shorba 34
Adrak ka aachar 226
Adrak-walla chapli kabab 122
Adrak-walli murgh 77
Aftari aloo 158–9
Aloo aur hari pati ka shorba 41
Aloo aur hari piyaz ki sabzi 135
Aloo chaat 146
Aloo mattar 136
Aloo phoolgobi mattar ki sabzi 141
Aloo qeema 123
Aloo tikki 144–5
Ambia ki chutni 222
Avocado aur tamatar ka sorba 37

Badam paparh 214
Bambai bhajya 26
Basmati pullao 185
Bathak mussallam 91
Bhare nimboo ka aachar 223–4
Bhuna adrak-walla gosht 127
Bhuna gosht 107–8
Bhuna phasli 115
Bhuni piyaz ke chaaval 184
Broccoli aur nimboo ka sorba 32
Broccoli ka aachar 217

Channa masaledar 198
Chapli kabab 121

Chilla aur chutni-walla murgh 75
Claverack ka khas gajar shorba 36

Dabba gosht 105–6
Dahi murgh 80, 81
Dahi-walla chap 113
Dahi-walla jhingha 64
Dahi-walli machli 47
Dahi-walli murgh kalejee 89
Darchini aur suwa-walla gajar 152
Darchini-walli dum naaspati 204
Dhokle 160–1
Dum ki lal machli 56

Feelmurgh mussallam 94
Feerni 213
Frazbeen sarsoon ke tail-walli 155–6

Gajjar ka aachar 221
Gajjar ka halva 202
Ganga Jumna subzi 148
Gayki boti 126
Gayki dum ki dal 196
Gobi tamatar 150
Gosht do piyaza 112
Gosht kabab 131

Hara masoor ki dal 191
Hara salaad 174
Hare patton ka salaad 165
Hari mirch nimboo ka aachar 219
Hari piyaz aur mirch-walli boti 118–19

Haridal ka salaad 164
Hindustani gazpacho 33

Ismail ka unde cachumber 99

Jhingha pullao 67–8

Kabuli chana 194
Kaju chaaval 187
Kaju gosht 128–9
Kali mirch murgh 86
Kashmiri gosht 130
Kashmiri qeema matter 124
Khagina 100–1
Khas aloo 137
Khas bathak masala 92
Khas feelmurgh ka masala 96
Khas unde 102
Kheera ka raita 139
Khopra poodina ki chutni 224–5
Kichri chaaval 181
Kishmishi lal karem kalle 154
Kothmiri unde roti 99
Kotmir illaichi-wale chaaval 179
Kumbhi akhroot ka salaad 166–7
Kumbhi dam ki machli 59
Kumbhi khas 138

Long-wale rasedar unde 98

Machli ka pullao 61
Machli ka salan 66
Machli ka tikka 57
Makai ke dane mirch-walli 149
Masala bhindi 157–8
Masale-walli rai murgh 83
Masaledar ananas 203
Masaledar gobi aloo 151
Masaledar lal karam kalle 153
Masaledar machli ke unde 48
Masaledar naryal salan 52
Masaledar sabzi 140
Masaledar tale pomfret 49
Masoor dal shorba 40
Masoor ka datcha 197
Mattar pullao 180
Meethe shaftaloo ki chutni 225–6
Meethi lassi 28
Meethi taheeri 210
Mirch aur kothmeer ka masala 74
Mirch aur tamatar ka salaad 173–4
Mirch-adrak-walla murgh mussallam 72
Moong dal 195
Motlabai sheekh kabab 125
Murgh kabab 79
Murgh korma 82
Murgh masala 88–9

Naaspati ka murabba 203–4
Namkeen lassi 28
Naryal jhinga masaledar 53
Naryal machli ka salan 50
Naryal-walla murgh 84
Nimboo adrak aur mirch ka murgh mussallam 73
Nimbu aur lasson-walli broccoli 155
Nimbu masoor dal 192–3

Palak bharta 142
Palak Jannu 143
Palak salaad 176
Paneer bhajya 25

Parveen ki tamatar chutni 218–9
Peela chaaval 186
Phal-walli qaaj mussallam 93
Phasli ka taj 114–5
Phoodina raita 175
Phool gobi ka aachar 227
Piston-walla raita 170

Qaaz mussallam 92–3
Qeema aloo tikki 119–20
Qeema masale-walla murgh 76
Qeema pullao 182
'Quartet' phal ka salaad 207

Rai adrak-walla bachra 132
Rai aur piyaz chingri chat 24
Rai aur suwa ki bhuni machli 54
Rai ke unde 101
Rai-walla boti gosht 106–7
Rai-walla jhingha 65
Rai-walli kumbhi 138
Rai-walli murgh kalejee 90
Rajasthani gosht 108
Richard ka khas murgh 87
Rogan josh 110

Sabji ka aachar 216–7
Sabzi-walla toast 147
Safaid gazpacho shorba 43
Safaid patte akhroot ka salaad 173
Santre ke chakle 205
Sareefe ki rabri 201
Sarson-walla jhingha 62
Sarsoon-walli asparagus 157
Seepdar machli aur naryal ka salan 51
Seerke-walli saljam 170
Shahi kofta 117–18
Shazeera-walla murgh mussallam 71
Shazeera-walla piyaz aur aloo ka salaad 172
Sheer khorma 208–9
Shemali gaye ke tukre baygan-walla 116
Shikampur machli 60
Shrikund 211
Sookhi patyoon ka aam-late 100
Soral shorba 39
Sukhi pati akhroot aur aloo ka salaad 171

Tali gilki 145
Tali hui machli 58
Tamatar aur piyaz ka salaad 166
Tamatar chutni 220
Tamatar gosht 109
Tamatar murgh 85
Tamatar shazeera-walla rasedar unde 97
Tamatar walli dum machli 55
Tandoori murgh 78
Tarbooj ki kheer 206
Taza kumbhi ka shorba 42
Taze sardine ki chat 27
Tej pati chaaval 186
Tez feelmurgh ka masala 95
Tez tamatar shorba 35
Tuna machli ka doosra salaad 168
Tuna machli ka pahela salaad 167
Tuna machli ka teesra salaad 169

Zafrani pullao 183
Zeera aur tamatar-walli rawas 63
Zeera mukhon-walli gilki 159